HOW THE
best INVEST

MAKE CONFIDENT DECISIONS
LIKE THE INVESTING SUPERSTARS

MALLIKA PAULRAJ

Praise

In a world where new or uncertain investors are inundated with avalanches of data, thought and opinions, *How the Best Invest* is a must-read. Mallika Paulraj has done a great job of dissecting and organizing the investment process. This book is filled with carefully curated nuggets that will help investors, unsure of investing, to develop a clear framework which will provide them with the confidence needed. Not a foolhardy confidence but one based on controlled thoughtfulness. Read, think and take control of your capital.

> — **Robert E. Robotti**, President and C.I.O., Robotti & Company

How the Best Invest is a brilliant exposition of the epistemology of investing and investors. It deftly distinguishes between what we know, what we think we know and what we merely profess to believe rather than admit to our own ignorance. It is a strongly flavorful distillation of modern investing practices made accessible to the individual investor.

> — **Dan diBartolomeo**, President and Owner, Northfield Information Services, Inc

Mallika has succeeded in writing a delightfully accessible, easy-to-understand book while covering a tremendous amount of ground. If you are looking to invest like the best investors in the world, this book will show you how. Very highly recommended!

— **John Mihaljevic**, C.F.A., Chairman, MOI Global

I have spent a couple of decades developing a circle of competence around one asset class (equities), focused in one geography (U.S.A.) for one simple reason: investing is very hard. If you don't focus on accumulating relevant knowledge and design a structured process for your day-to-day activities, you will fail. It is extremely refreshing to see someone, with the experience and outstanding analytical skill as Mallika, saying something similar. Investors that have assets to protect – and hopefully grow – will benefit immensely by using the mental models and frameworks provided by this book. The investing journey is long, arduous and full of pitfalls: Mallika will help you reach the other side.

— **Danilo Santiago**, Founding Partner at Rational Investment Methodology

Angel investors are spoilt for choice these days with innumerable investment opportunities open to them. Mallika's book proposes a systematic way of making investment decisions in the face of countless investment opportunities.

— **Susanne Chishti**, C.E.O., FINTECH Circle and Co-Editor of the FINTECH, WEALTHTECH and INSURTECH books

How the Best Invest beautifully distils the author's extensive first-hand expertise as a successful practitioner and with a refreshingly accessible voice is a sheer delight to read. A treasure trove of insights, for the novice and professional alike!

    — **Shai Dardashti**, Founder, Casulo Group

The beauty of Mallika's book lies in putting the investor in the center of the action. Investing itself does not change much in time. It remains the same. The secret of mastering it lies in the knowledge of oneself and in the study of investment giants. This is Mallika's path, and we readers follow her, too.

    — **Daniel Gladiš**, Director, Vltava Fund

Mallika's book needed to be written. In a sea of investing fog and confusion, Mallika provides the reader with a lighthouse for how to organize your financial life and make superior, rational decisions. *How the Best Invest* lifts the weight from the shoulders of all of those who are stressed by the myriad of financial choices facing them. A must read.

    — **Gary Mishuris**, C.F.A., Managing Partner and
      C.I.O., Silver Ring Value Partners

Mallika, a deeply quantitative computer programmer, stumbled into the investing world in the late 90s and has written about her experience of investing and advising about it. The difference to other investment books is that it condenses two decades of investment experience in nine chapters including asset allocation, behavioral biases, checklists mixed with her fun and casual life wisdom. A must-read fast forward to the investing start line with a compass to know where to run to!

— **Christian Freischütz**, Value School

RETHINK PRESS

For my best investments:
Indira and Amara

Contents

Introduction

In God we trust. Everybody else brings data to
the table.
    — Narayana Murthy

The Hindus believe in the concept of Trimurti –
three (tri) idols (murti) who govern the cyclicality
of the Universe:

- Brahma, the force of Creation

- Vishnu, the force of Preservation

- Shiva, the force of Destruction

All things in life are in one of the three stages, moving
inevitably to the next stage.

This makes sense in the investing world. Companies are born with a brilliant entrepreneurial idea. They grow and become mainstream, their economic viability preserved by a vast army of employees. Then, as the world changes, inevitably their time is over and they go into decline. At this point of destruction, either the company recreates itself with new ideas and technology, or another company emerges to take its place.

For example, the Ford Motor Company, started in 1903, was created out of years of learning around internal combustion engines. In the 20th century it had a dominant role in motorizing our lives with cars and trucks. It now struggles to maintain market position and must reinvent itself with cleaner technologies and changing transportation trends such as self-driving cars and on-demand taxis.

In 2017 only *one* company, General Electric, remained from the original Dow Jones Index, created in 1896 to list the largest U.S. companies. General Electric was booted out that year, and by 2018 every single one of the original Dow Jones companies had been absorbed by later-born competitors. One of these original companies had created leather tool belts for workers. It disappeared without a trace as soon as automation took hold of the economy at the dawn of the 20th century. One can predict that by 2120, only a handful of today's seemingly unbeatable beasts such as Apple,

Amazon and Goldman Sachs will remain. History predicts that even Google will be gone.

Whole industries are in the creation-preservation-destruction cycle. When an industry fails, or a stock collapses, we're just seeing a cycle end. From it will come a rebirth and a new creation. We can position our investment portfolio to stack the decks against destruction and take advantage of the forces of creation and preservation. Against this backdrop of investment cycles, we make investment decisions about what we do with our money.

There's an inside joke in the investment management world that you cannot have a client presentation without a well-designed graph that slopes upwards to the right, showing how the client's money will grow. If you can't tell the story of the graph sloping upwards in time, why bother showing up to work? Making decisions on investing is a process of listening to stories and deciding which one is most likely. There are some credible investment managers out there who will tell the story of the graph sloping upwards, and some terrible, even dishonest ones who tell similar stories. The only way to sort out the credible stories from the untrue is to look at the data that underlies them. Nothing counts but evidence and numbers. We must make sure we are bringing the right investing stories, backed by data, to the table.

How I figured out investing

Investing wasn't always my goal in life. I had an excellent education courtesy of the academically-minded family I was born into. I went to Stanford and the London School of Economics and studied investing at London Business School. From 1997 to the present, I have worked in the world's centers of business – Silicon Valley, Wall Street and London's The City.

My background is deeply quantitative and research-based. I started my career as a computer programmer for companies in Silicon Valley, and then stumbled into a programming job in investment banking in New York. I've worked for Lehman Brothers, Morgan Stanley Capital International and several fund managers and investment research firms. I was moving billions of dollars around on a spreadsheet and saying all kinds of glamorous things about it and writing intense research reports, but I couldn't take $100,000 and know what to do with it in the market. That's why I call myself an accidental investor. I didn't set out with the goal of making lots of money; I randomly walked into the investment industry.

I could model complex financial instruments on spreadsheets, but I couldn't make fundamental investing decisions such as what investing strategy to pick for myself or how to select a wealth manager.

With a view to filling in the gaps in my investing knowledge, I interviewed a number of wealth managers, but they didn't tell me anything new. No one was telling me what I really needed to know. At that point it occurred to me that if those smart people didn't know what to do, if they were stuck, basically I was stuck too.

Then a professor friend of mine who was a successful investor in addition to his academic career, recommended I research the area of value investing. It was a Damascus moment. Value investing is what American business magnate, speaker and philanthropist Warren Buffett does, and it has made him one of the most successful investors in the world. John Templeton, Peter Lynch, and Seth Klarman – many of the famous investors who enjoyed success decade after decade, used this investing approach.

Essentially, value investing looks at companies that are going to gain value over a long period. The value investing approach of buying good quality investments when they are lower in price to what they are worth and then patiently waiting for the price to go up can be used in other investment areas such as property. I've achieved success in this world, and everything I've learned has come from reading, listening and speaking to the world's greatest investors.

Back to basics

> Don't sell anything you wouldn't buy yourself.
> — Charlie Munger

I've taken a gamble that I will serve the world and myself well by teaching people to make better investing decisions. Practical, non-academic education is what the investment world needs. Since launching my blog *Four Minute Investing* based on timeless principles used by the world's greatest investors, I've acquired a number of investment coaching clients, including several wealthy families. I've been a guest speaker at some of the best business schools and conducted investment management seminars.

Through my client work, workshops, reading, and speaking to countless professional investors, I've recognized a pattern emerging – a useful framework for individual self-sufficient investors: control, self-assurance, clearness and tranquility. That said, although I discuss a lot of companies and investors in this book, I am not affiliated with anyone. I'm not promoting any one firm or fund manager; I simply mention people as examples.

Decisions

To invest your money is to confront an endless series of decisions. Should you outsource the process or do it yourself? Will you be an active or passive investor? Should you buy real estate or go into the stock market?

The harsh reality of investing is that it can leave you dazed and confused. Time is short and the pile of documents to go through is high. How do you choose a wealth manager or fund manager? Beyond stocks and bonds, should you investigate all the fancy options on offer? How do you divide your money across different continents? Is the United States safer than Asia, or will Asia give you better returns over a decade? What sectors do you think will win? Technology is booming, but are utility companies more reliable? What about all the new-fangled artificial intelligence (A.I.) mobilized portfolio apps? Do you rely on plain old human common sense?

People beat themselves up because they've lost money, not made as much money as they *should* have, or haven't done anything at all with their money. Many end up carrying cash for years on end, unwilling to mentally leave behind investments that went badly years ago. If any of the questions or descriptions in this section find resonance within you, please read on. If you feel stuck in your investment decisions, you have in your hands the right book for you.

1

The Complex Investment World

It's all part of my journey – I've done a lot of stupid things, but you learn by your mistakes.
— Ozzy Osbourne

Investing your money is a double-edged sword. On the one hand, it's good to be an investor and have many options ahead of you. But whether you've sold a company, won a large bonus or inherited wealth, the burden of investing and managing your money can weigh heavily on your shoulders. There are many expectations that you will do this well. You may have charitable obligations to meet, children you want to pass wealth on to or ambitions to grow your influence in the world. The responsibility of putting money to work always brings with it the risk of losing it, and the embarrassment, pain and sense of letting people down that would accompany that loss. Investors only tend to talk about their successes, so it's hard to learn from failures unless you make them yourself.

For those of us who are lucky enough to have money to invest, there are two main parts to the problem of being under-confident about investment decision making:

1. Our brain

2. The structure of the investing world

Given the human brain's aversion to loss and attraction to shiny things, we oscillate between glee and despair. We stay frozen, unable and unwilling to act on our investment dreams, or we stay within the confines of where we feel safe. Lessons from our parents and conditioning from our cultures affect the money stories we tell ourselves. I've watched my family and friends make and then lose so much money through bad decisions, it's taken me twenty-plus years and working with some of the elite names in the finance industry to trust my ability around investment.

The investing world is complex, bordering on chaotic. We are inundated by financial news stories about why a company moved up or down within a day, when for most of us the investing process is far longer than one gyration in the market. Smartphones have exacerbated this problem with an avalanche of data constantly hitting our investing news apps. You and I can access financial information from corporate giants and providers such as Bloomberg that a few years ago was available only to professional asset managers. We are constantly checking our 'numbers', and in that process losing their context in our holistic financial wellbeing. The debacle of Bernie Madoff, where hundreds of investors and charities were taken in, has made people less comfortable with 'social proof', where a trusted friend investing with someone who also appeared to get fabulous returns may have seemed like a foolproof decision. Horror stories such as Madoff and the 2008 financial crisis have reduced people's trust in their own investing decisions.

The good news and the bad news

The good news is that today is the best time in history to be an investor. If you have assets you want to grow, the choices you have would have made your parents' heads reel. Warren Buffett only made his first investment outside the United States in the 1990s, but for an investor starting out today, it would be unusual to confine yourself to just one country. What was impossible ten years ago is two swipes away today. You can sit in Texas and buy a slice of a real-estate project in India. You can buy physical gold, from choosing your bars to where to store it, on your laptop from the website of the 1,000-year-old Royal Mint. You can buy and sell assets from Myanmar to Massachusetts from an app on your phone.

A combination of research and the power of computing has given rise to a dizzying array of investing innovations and options. Big data and the ease of graphical user interfaces on our computer screens and phones means anyone can buy and sell sophisticated investments. We no longer need access to a broker cordoned off behind a velvet rope of elitism or an investment bank to know the 'codes' to access certain investments. Even highly complicated structured products such as collateralized loan obligations (C.L.O.s) and derivatives can now be bought for a few thousand dollars. Regulators have become increasingly watchful, too, using sophisticated tools and rules to protect the system against rogue investors. The Galleon case of insider trading, for example, was brought to trial because a computer algorithm detected an anomaly in trading patterns.

In addition to the democratization of investments and the smaller ticket size for admission into this world, the way to monitor and risk manage your investments is also becoming more accessible. Blogs and models produced by clever investors make it easier to innovate. The superstars of the investing world such as Warren Buffett and Ray Dalio, who I believe truly want to help normal investors, share their thinking with you directly via websites, video, current holdings or books. And technology is easing the way too. Instead of you having to calculate signals such as the price to earnings ratio, these come automatically and freely attached to the Google search results of a company.

The bad news is that today is the most overwhelming time in history to be an investor. With the vast amount of investing choices before us, it's hard to know where to start or who to believe. The rate of change is getting faster with the rise of Fintech startups and A.I. portfolio construction taking us away from the simplicity of picking a single stock or company. The logo of the company and the current share price is lurking on your screen and all you have to do is press buy. Or should you sell? There are too many options, too many decisions to make.

Investment is heavily regulated by the governments (as it should be), but financial news services on investing are not regulated. A news commentator can make up whatever story they want, and to keep the audience coming back, they will add to the story every day. Conversely, fund managers who often know exactly what's going on are extremely careful about what they say and how they give advice. It is difficult, if not impossible, to know what's truly going on, unless you've built a credible network to consult.

Most wealth managers are relationship managers, not money managers. There is nothing unethical about this; their job is to win the client. But how many wealth managers truly understand all the jargon surrounding asset allocation and risk management and stock picking of the underlying funds?

Also, we now realize that *no one*, not even the best investment manager, knows anything in a moment of crisis, such as Lehman Brothers Holdings Inc., the fourth largest investment bank in the United States, filing for bankruptcy in 2008, the tragedy of 9/11 or the uncertainty of Brexit. They can only position themselves beforehand to react to market upsets and do their best to make sense of things as the situation evolves. All this increasing complication can cause us as investors to become overwhelmed and trapped by inaction or anxiety.

The burden on individual investors

In this new world of inundation by financial products and the resultant increase in investment duties each of us must shoulder, there will be victors, and there will be victims. We must now learn how to make decisions that previously we could have delegated. The burden is on us to pay more attention to investments and how we select them. The bank or investment firm we choose today may not be around for decades. The relationship manager we have most certainly won't be.

The risk lies with us.

The victors in this emerging age of investing will be those of us who can tame our brains to have a growth mindset, believing in our capability to learn and change. Those who invest for the long term (three to five years minimum) and study the great investors will win. Those of us who educate ourselves and seek the right professionals to outsource to, once we understand at a fundamental level how the markets work, will rule the 21st century world of investments.

The victims of these enormous changes in the investing world will be those who cede control to others without understanding the underlying strategies. The ones who chase the next new fad in day trading, stock picks or startups without having a personal investment decision-making framework. Victims will be the ones who instead of carefully investigating the latest investment fashions stay fearful in the silos of what they know. The ones who have outsourced their investments yet remain angry at the fees of their fund managers. Investors with 'return envy' who want to make a fast buck like they were told their friend or brother-in-law did. An investor who will lose in this new reality will be the one who allows themselves to be inundated by financial news, forever on their phone looking at investing news and apps without a clear framework of how to use these tools and data.

Despite the greater burden of having to be responsible for our investments, we also now have greater power than we did before thanks to the knowledge and easy-to-use tech-based investing tools we have available. Many bad investing decisions can be avoided simply by asking the right questions.

A fresh, systematic approach to investing

This book outlines an easy-peasy version of the approach that has proven useful time and time again with my clients. In my coaching practice, I start clients off by getting them to ask themselves these five questions. Don't feel you need to know the answers right now; these are just the base questions you need to navigate the waters of investing:

- How much of your wealth do you want to manage yourself, and how much do you want to outsource to others?

- How much do you want to be divided between real assets and virtual assets? Real assets include rental properties or gold coins – things you can see and touch that need looking after. Virtual assets include stocks and bonds, which you can manage while sitting on a beach.

- What investments do you think will do well in the next twenty to thirty years? Why do you believe that? Do you only 'believe' it, or have you done the relevant analysis?

- Do you have a written checklist to analyze any investment proposal offered you?

- Have you scheduled time into your busy life to educate yourself about investing?

The most powerful way I've found of learning how to be a good investor is to study the superstar investors of the world. Their timeless principles rely more on common sense than on complex equations. Many of them follow the concept of value investing, which needs a long-term mindset.

I'm going to propose a simple framework for successfully investing your own money and how to deal with market anxiety. I'll start by explaining why it's so difficult to be a confident investor in today's market, then I'll take you through the Superinvestar Framework – Control, Confidence, Clarity, Calm and Checklists.

More than anything else, there are three things I want you to take away from this book:

1. Think about investing your money on a long-term basis – three to five years at a minimum.

2. Put yourself at the center of the investing decision-making process. Make the investment industry work for you rather than passively waiting for someone else to diagnose what you need.

3. Instead of making decisions without context, follow a step-by-step process.

My aim for this book is for it to be the book I wish I'd had at the very beginning – a book that starts with the right questions.

Further steps

- How much of your wealth do you manage yourself, how much do you outsource?

- How much do you want to be divided between real assets and virtual assets?

- What investment themes do you think will do well in the next twenty to thirty years?

- What is your current process for evaluating a new investment idea?

- What makes you say yes to a new investing idea? What makes you say no?

2
Why Investing Is So Hard

A V.U.C.A. world – volatile, uncertain, complex and
ambiguous.
— The U.S. Army War College

V.U.C.A. is a concept that the U.S. Army War
College originated to describe the volatility,
uncertainty, complexity and ambiguity of managing
warfare to its officers. Although it's now slightly
overused in business planning, I'm going to stick my
neck out and use it here as it captures the investing
landscape nicely. Even though your portfolio might
load onto your computer screen with structured
boxes, clean numbers and coordinating colors, the
world of investing is:

- Volatile – markets go up and down like stomach-churning roller coasters.

- Uncertain – what held in 1980 (gasoline-based cars) does not hold in 2020 (Tesla, Uber, etc.).

- Complex – with geographic, technological, economic and political inputs, investing cannot be modelled precisely.

- Ambiguous – what is a startup worth? Why did the Amazon share price move up or down today?

Investing is simple, but not easy

A diet plan is simple. You eat less of the bad foods, more of the good foods. What do you do to be healthy and lose weight? You eat properly, exercise, drink your green juice and swallow your vitamins. And yet, so many people (including me) struggle to remain fit as it's hard to do. A healthy diet and an exercise regime are logical, but our brains can struggle to make the right choices. It's simple, but not easy.

In this respect, investing is like dieting and losing weight – so much so that Richard Oldfield, executive chairman of his family's investment company Oldfield Partners, called his book about investing *Simple But Not Easy*. We should buy low and sell high. It's a simple strategy. We could go out, read books on the subject and start building our portfolio. We could ask friends to refer us to a good wealth manager, but instead, many of us find ourselves trying to make complicated decisions in sticky situations.

There are two main reasons for this. The first relates to how the human brain has evolved to work. The second is the result of how investing news and data spread.

Fighting your inner chimp

We human beings are nothing more than glorified chimps. Pretend now that you are a chimp in the jungle. Swinging away through the trees, you collect a load of bananas. You can't eat all the bananas today, so you're standing there with your arms full, wondering what to do with them. How do you save them for another day?

Another chimp comes along and offers to grow your stash of bananas for you. She shows you a lovely hole in the ground ringed by palm leaves. All you need to do is drop your bananas into the hole and leave them with your new best chimp friend.

'Come back in a few years,' she says, 'and I'll have double the number of bananas for you.' But while she's speaking, the trees are ringing with the cries of chimps who have lost their bananas.

Your instinctual brain locks up and screams, 'No, don't take my bananas away from me.' This is a primal response, and it's why we procrastinate on investing decisions. Our inaction then causes anxiety because we know we should be doing something, but we don't.

Take a deep breath. The human brain needs a long time to trust something and is highly loss averse. It's not your fault – it's just the way your brain is wired to protect you. Relax. You're merely following your instincts.

Your brain on investing

> To survive and pass on their genes, our ancestors needed to be especially aware of dangers, losses and conflicts. Consequently, the brain evolved a negativity bias that looks for bad news, reacts intensely to it, and quickly stores the experience in neural structure.
> — Rick Hanson, author of *Hardwiring Happiness*

We human beings are just slightly more evolved chimps. Our brains process decisions, including investing ones, in an evolutionary hierarchy.

Below is a stylized diagram of the brain. Our human brain has evolved from a reptilian brain into our current, much more complex human brain.

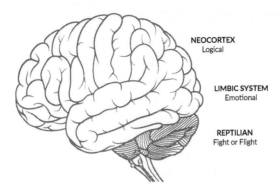

NEOCORTEX
Logical

LIMBIC SYSTEM
Emotional

REPTILIAN
Fight or Flight

First, we have the reptilian or primal brain that controls us with a fight or flight response. The poor chimp, when confronted with the banana decision, freezes in fear or runs away from deciding. At this point in our investment decisions, we take in information through the reptilian brain – we've evolved that way, so there's not much we can do to change it. And this leads to a similar fight or flight response to the chimps. The reptilian brain is a 'yes/no' 'enemy/friend' contraption that either reacts or freezes, depending on its programming.

The next level of the evolutionary brain is the limbic system or emotional brain that views the banana decision as an overwhelming conflict. The chimp wants more bananas while wanting to keep the ones he or she already has safe. This results in anxiety.

The limbic system is the part of the brain that might look at a piece of pumpkin pie and go, 'Oh, pumpkin pie. Yum, yum,' and want to eat it. At the same time, this causes anxiety as the emotional brain knows the pumpkin pie is fattening and there's a weigh-in at the gym the next day.

Lastly, we have the logical brain or neocortex, which executes the wonderful powers of analysis we humans have. This third part of our brain is what evolved to make us human.

Based on my simplified explanation of neuroscience, where do you think your investing decision should be made? Which part of the brain? Any stimulus approaching the human brain is first processed via the reptilian system, then it flows through to the limbic system where it causes us to feel happy or sad or anxious. It finally reaches our neocortex, our logical thinking structures, which is of course where investing decisions should be made. But the poor brain is often so caught up in the fear and anxiety from its primal part and limbic system that it rarely gets to use the power of logic.

If we buy an investment and it goes up, we feel happy. Yay! If it goes down, we berate ourselves or blame our money manager, or we don't do anything because the reptile brain has stuck the 'I'm frozen' label on the door like a sulky teenager and is refusing to engage.

Does any of this sound familiar to you in your investing life?

The professional and the amateur

It's not supposed to be easy. Anyone who finds it
easy is stupid.
    — Charlie Munger

Meet fund manager Jane. She is forty-five, highly edu-
cated and a senior investor concentrating on U.S. tech
at a respected Wall Street firm.

Jane wakes up in the morning and arrives at her desk
to discover things are moving in the markets, and in
the wrong direction. She calmly decides what stocks
her team needs to investigate and assigns research
accordingly. Next, she has a chat with the sales and
marketing guys on how they will handle jittery investment clients that day.

By lunchtime, her researchers are back. They chat
for two hours, and by the end of the day, Jane has
decided what she needs to trim, what she needs to
buy more of, and how to position her fund against
the market sell-off. She can't sell and go to cash as,
like many asset managers, the terms with her investors mean she can only hold a maximum of 5% of
their investments in cash.

A cool $100 million has landed in her fund's account
from a pension fund she has been courting for years,
but since Jane can't hold cash, even in the scary markets, she deploys the new capital immediately.

Jane leaves the office. It's been a hard day, but she has acted on all the problems facing her fund and made the best decisions she can. Jane is a professional.

Jane then goes to dinner and happens to be seated next to Mallika. On hearing Mallika helps people make better investment decisions, she signs right up to one of Mallika's seminars.

'I need help making decisions,' says Jane. 'My investments are a mess.'

Mallika has heard this many times before. Jane is acting like an amateur, but only when it comes to her own money. She has too many choices. Should she go to cash or go to bonds? Quit her job and flee to Timbuktu? Put this year's bonus into the startup she likes? Her emotions are too strong when it comes to her own money.

I started my business to help smart professionals and entrepreneurs. After my many years of working in finance, most of my contacts were also in finance, and I was surprised to find out how many of them were having trouble managing their finances and making decisions.

Why do finance professionals act like amateurs when it comes to investing their own money? When they are at work, they make decisions out of their logical brain. They are well trained, they know how to act, they have colleagues to speak to and outsource hard decisions to, they have a set of constraints to work within. With their own finances, they have strong emotions surrounding the topic. They know they need to invest but are almost paralyzed by the wealth of information available on asset allocation, stock picking and the latest investing trends. Unlike laypeople, they don't believe in one person or fund's ability to get everything right; they know they need to understand things for themselves and outsource accordingly, but they are too close to the casino randomness of the markets and their reptile brain freezes.

The amoeba dance

An amoeba is a single-celled organism that doesn't have a brain. It just responds to stimuli around it and moves reactively. This is a good representation of what many of us are like in our investing lives. We're being reactive, doing an amoeba dance.

Imagine something great happens to Amazon's share price. If you own Amazon shares, you're happy. Then you hear that California house prices have gone down, and since you own real estate there, you become discouraged. News about interest rates from the U.S. Federal Reserve or the Bank of England sends you askew, depending on whether you think it's a threat or benefit to your portfolio. Soon you get bent out of shape, reacting rather than being organized and deliberate.

We all as investors face the universal handicap about how to deal with market anxiety. Why then is it so difficult to nudge our brain from fight or flight to a more logical way of thinking?

The human brain doesn't like change. From an evolutionary perspective, it holds onto things it has invested time and energy into, and it's wary of new things. People often share their investment thoughts with me. And usually, they are stressed by having to change something, end something or start something new.

For example, they tell me:

- I should sell my shares in company X and reinvest
- I have too many brokerage accounts, I only need one
- I really should move some money back to the United States from Hong Kong
- I need to find my pension paperwork for my job from 2003 and move the money
- I should kill the bank account in Cambodia

That's just a snapshot of the kind of things I hear every day. These cycles of 'I really should...' thoughts take up mental space and keep us from moving forward in our investment goals. It is exhausting being a dancing amoeba.

Parental conditioning

When you're making investing decisions for yourself, yours isn't the only voice in your head. Your parents educate and inform your attitudes towards saving, spending and risk (I'm using a two-parent family for illustrative purposes only). As you go through life, your experiences and the economy you work in contribute to shaping your individual views. If you're making decisions with your spouse, then their parents' views and life experiences all come into play too. How is the divorce rate not higher than 50%?

The areas of conflict that people experience when making investment decisions can be broadly categorized as the differences in what they perceive as valuable and what they consider risky. I'll share two short stories as examples.

WHAT WE VALUE

I think $500 is a reasonable amount to spend on a handbag. In the London financial markets where I work, most of my female colleagues consider me a cheapskate. Hermes, Celine, Chanel and Louis Vuitton sell bags starting at over $2,000, and that's the norm for women who work in The City or Wall Street.

My mother thinks about $100 is the right price for a handbag. Something practical and solid, not fashionable like the ones I splurge on. My father can't understand why women must schlep around so much stuff, and if we must carry it, why can't we use a five-cent plastic bag that the groceries come in?

Three people, three differing perspectives on the value of things, three voices in my head.

WHAT WE CONSIDER RISKY

A while ago, a Swedish colleague married a nice English girl. They're both established in jobs in London and ready for a life together, but they can't agree on buying a house.

The Swedes, despite their cozy communal spirit and a population of just a few million, managed to give themselves a financial housing crisis that saw house prices plummet 40%–50% in 1992. My friend remembers his parents working for years to pay a mortgage that was underwater. His English wife has only seen house prices rising, and to her buying an apartment is an investment decision that is as 'safe as houses'.

Different life experiences, different perspectives on how risky an investment is.

Financial news and data overwhelm

The greatest distortion to our ability to think clearly around investing is the financial news and data we encounter constantly. This impairs our ability to understand the markets long term and make investing decisions. On our screens, we keep seeing that the stock market is up, the stock market is down, this thing is blowing up, this company is bankrupt. We have so much data bombarding us through our smartphones.

In the 1960s, Warren Buffett started making a name for himself. One of his key methods of trouncing the competition (arbitrage) was knowing what companies were doing before the stockbrokers in New York did. In her book *The Snowball: Warren Buffett and the Business of Life*, biographer Alice Schroeder shares stories about Buffett getting on a train to physically visit the companies he was following. He knew when the financial reports were due and would get a copy before it was bound and mailed to New York. Buffett was then able to quickly process whether a company was doing well or not and make his buy/sell/hold decision long before his peers. He claimed that this diligence gave him an investing edge for many years.

In the 1990s, when I was working in Silicon Valley, I had a project to list C.E.O.s in the tech sector, which meant finding a copy of the *Businessweek* magazine in my university library to come up with the latest set of C.E.O. names. By the time I found the article I needed, photocopied it and typed out the names, that was a day gone. Today within seconds, I can view a list of C.E.O.s worldwide on my phone. A further click brings me biographies, dates of birth and other information. Two clicks later, I can be listening to a talk by a C.E.O. who catches my eye or reading an article they have written.

In the same way, financial information dissemination is now nearly instant. Algorithms written by high-frequency traders can catch movements long before the human brain can process the same information. The stock market is revalued every few seconds. A large company can go up or down in value by a billion dollars based on a tweet by a blogger that isn't based on any fundamental change in the strategy or sales of the company.

Newspapers must have news to sell every day – that is their business model. So what if the news for them today is that the market went up? And then tomorrow, the news is that the market went down. Your brain could be taking in all the ups and downs of the market from one news channel. Newspapers and television also love to glorify bad news as it is much more interesting than good news. A C.E.O. scandal or fraud is much more interesting to report on than a company that does what it says it's going to and keeps growing by doing just that.

There's a lot of data coming at our chimp brains, and we need to see the enduring picture rather than being reactive. I find it's useful to think of financial news as 'guesses'. Company share prices are the result of a complex interaction of overall economic sentiment, company news and competitor news. A financial journalist writing about or explaining a share price movement isn't giving you data; they are guessing as to why the valuation went up or down. And anyone who predicts what will happen tomorrow is also just guessing.

> Wise men speak because they have something to say; fools because they have to say something.
> — Plato

It is essential to take a step back regularly to see things clearly. Treat those numbers on your phone, giving you all the share and index prices, as guesses rather than data, and you'll save yourself a lot of grief.

What's a chimp to do? How do you take your investing decisions out of inaction (reptilian brain) and anxiety (emotional brain) and move them into your logical brain? The Superinvestar Framework, which I will introduce in the next chapter, is designed to help you move to a state of knowledgeable action. As fun as it's been to spend time in the treetops with the chimps and their bananas, it's time now to get down to a step-by-step approach of moving our investing selves up the evolutionary tree.

Further steps

- Think back to your last investment opportunity. What part of your brain did you use most?

- How has your parents' attitude towards money shaped your investments?

- What was your worst investment ever? Does the memory still influence your decisions today?

- Book suggestion: *Thinking, Fast And Slow* by Daniel Kahneman.

- Book suggestion: *The Little Book of Behavioral Investing: How Not to be Your Own Worst Enemy* by James Montier.

3
The Superinvestar Framework

Water, water, everywhere,
Nor any drop to drink.
— Samuel Coleridge, *Rime of the Ancient Mariner*

Where do you start learning about investing? The *New York Times* personal finance column? The *Financial Times*? News apps? Websites? Bloomberg? CNBC? The market moves up; the market moves down. The media does not teach you investment decision making.

Wealth managers, financial advisors, investment managers? There are some great ones out there who do the right things, but their model is to take your money and make investing decisions for you. They are not in the business to educate you. They already follow a system they refined long before you came along.

Friends and family? Your professional network? They might have interesting real-estate ventures you can invest in together, but they don't have a holistic picture of your investing life. Although they can advise on an investment, they can't tell you if it's right for you or how much of your entire collection of assets to invest.

Books? You could read twenty books and become a good investor. Most of my knowledge comes from my love of reading investment books, but I know many people do not have time to do this. That is one of the reasons I decided to simplify my learnings and put them together in this one book.

How do you learn to be a better investor? How do you get past the fear and the struggle and the knowledge barriers? A step-by-step investing framework is what you need.

Advantages of a framework

The old masters of painting, such as Rembrandt and Goya, would often commission a customized frame to complement their masterpieces. For example, if there was a forest scene depicted in the painting, then the frame might incorporate leaves and acorns, carved into the wood and then gilded. The master artists recognized the advantages of concentrating on the framework around a piece of art because:

- It holds the artwork in place
- It displays and accentuates the artwork
- If the artwork doesn't fit the frame, viewers can tell right away

What are the advantages of focusing on the framework in which you invest?

- It gives you a structure to hang your investments on
- You have somewhere to start in evaluating any investment opportunity thrown at you
- If it doesn't fit, you realize immediately

The easiest way to have a framework for your investments is to make a simple list of things to consider. I'm constantly surprised that even professional investors rarely stop to think of the bigger picture. They go along with what their predecessors or their firms tell them to do.

Introducing the 5 Cs

Throughout my years of coaching and mentoring wealthy individuals, I have developed a system called the Superinvestar Framework, which aims to help investors structure their learning and habits. It consists of the 5 Cs for reducing anxiety and increasing action.

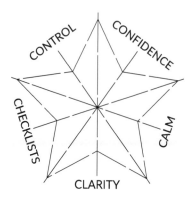

I will now outline the 5 Cs briefly, and will subsequently devote a chapter to each C.

Control

When it comes to their investing lives, people dream of both being able to do it all themselves and finding the magic bullet, either person or company, that can do it all for them. The only way to be effective is to put yourself at the center of your investing life, treating investment advisors and wealth managers as service providers, so the first C stands for Control. This C moves you from the mindset of the dancing amoeba to creating and following coherent plans, which are like spokes in a wheel with you at the center.

I'm not advocating that you become a do-it-yourself (D.I.Y.) investor; I merely ask that you shift your thinking to see yourself as in charge of the process. You understand what the wealth manager or the advisor is doing with your money. You understand their strategy and fees. You understand what returns they can obtain for you and what risks they are taking with your money.

Controlling your time and mindset is the only thing you can have power over in investing. Market forces create their own chaotic and unpredictable whirl. The next chapter will take you through the basic steps to moving forward from past mistakes and controlling your time and attention span.

Confidence

The second C in the Superinvestar Framework stands for Confidence. Confidence in your investment decision making stems from having the right knowledge and taking action.

Why not learn from the best investors in the world, the superstars such as Warren Buffett? In Chapter 5, we will learn how the best invest and align our tactics and mindset to follow some of their principles from our laptop. We will also look at what long-term investing research, looking back over decades, has taught us about the best investments. The average fund manager shows us a few quarters of performance when pitching us their services. What if we went back further? What holds up over the long haul?

Calm

The right action and the right investments can only come about if you have a peaceful mind and a grounded way of thinking, so the third C is Calm. We'll look in Chapter 6 at documented strategies of well-known professional investors and see how they stay calm in white-knuckle markets. It is all in your mind.

Clarity

The fourth C in the Superinvestar Framework stands for Clarity. Success in investing over decades demands that you know what kind of portfolio you want and what steps to take towards it.

Often, potential investors go to the markets saying, 'Tell me what I should do,' and the markets will always have a different answer, depending on who they're talking to. You need to go to the investing marketplace with a clear idea of what you want and how the investing 'recipes' work. Chapter 7, the chapter on Clarity, details how you can make the decision rather than the decision being pushed onto you. It also introduces you to ice-cream sundae investing, my take on how to approach the difficult problem of asset allocation.

Checklists

Airplane pilots worldwide use checklists before take-off to make sure they have covered all the things that could go wrong. In Chapter 8, we will discuss the fifth and final C, Checklists.

We use checklists in our daily lives, but we rarely apply them to investing. In Chapter 8, I will outline a list of things you need to think about, a checklist to complete before you allow an investment to be made. It's essential for successfully investing your own money, but generic enough to cover most scenarios, whether you're going to the stock market or funding a friend's business.

Now, let's dive into the first C: controlling your investments.

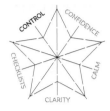

4

Control – Put Yourself At The Center

The most difficult thing is the decision to act; the rest is merely tenacity...
— Amelia Earhart

Take back your power

Imagine you had Warren Buffett sitting in your living room every night doing your investing for you. Even if you had this investing superhero at your service, you would have to understand his strategy to invest confidently. You would have to understand the choices he was making for you and why he was making those choices. Human nature can't just allow anyone, even the world's greatest investor, to set and forget when it comes to wealth. Even though he has millions of investors, Warren Buffett still writes his annual letter, runs a huge annual meeting, and constantly explains and defends his investing decisions. Even the master is questioned – and rightly so.

If Warren Buffett's investors feel the need to question him annually, what about you and your sense of control over your investments? By control, I do not mean you have to become a D.I.Y. investor. There are many excellent wealth-management platforms and advisors out there, as well as people who manage every penny for themselves. But by putting yourself in the center of your decision making and gaining control, you make your choices deliberately. You choose a wealth manager whose strategy you understand and approve of, or you choose to take some or all of your assets and invest them yourself.

Starting over

The more I speak to people, the more I realize that most folks have a lot of trouble making investment decisions. They are stuck in analysis paralysis and never press the go button. Like I have done myself in the past, they spin into a cycle of procrastination, followed by doubt.

Maslow's Hierarchy of Needs[1] is a popular framework often used in psychology to explain the inbuilt priorities we human beings place on our needs. At the base, the highest priority, are our physiological needs (water, food, sleep). Once these are taken care of, we cover our physical safety needs, followed by belonging to a loving group, feelings of self-esteem and accomplishment, and finally self-actualization needs: achieving our full potential. Investing decisions are essentially long-term decisions and not a matter of immediate survival. As such, they take place in the top part of the Maslow hierarchy, in the esteem and self-actualization states. At that level you are feeling secure enough to commit to the uncertain future of investing. But if your job or health is under threat, or your portfolio is suffering from a major stock market upheaval, it is difficult to rise above the physiological and safety states.

Where are you currently in the hierarchy? Are you in the right states for investing? Are your basic needs being met?

In my work with clients, I'll often find people who are still stuck in poor investing decisions they committed to years ago, or perhaps they remember their parents being sideswiped by a catastrophic decision. Surely, we're better off starting by knowing there are innate human biases that can prevent us from making the best investments for the long term.

---

1   Maslow, A.H., 'A theory of human motivation.' *Psychological Review.* 50 [4] (1943), p370–96.

Aim for 'good enough' investing

Have you ever watched the Olympics? It can be brutal watching the young athletes compete. We feel happy for the euphoric winners, but so sorry for the 'losers'. I became obsessed with the Olympics as an eight-year-old, having been taken to the 1984 Los Angeles Games. I dreamed of cycling or swimming to victory. Those dreams died young!

There is only one gold, one silver and one bronze. Beyond those three categories, everyone else is an also-ran. Although the running ability of the person who comes last in the Olympic 100-meter race is vastly superior to any athletic ability most people have, we will never hear their name or how much they trained and gave of their minds and bodies.

It's our human tendency to want to be the best. We are a species set up in a system where the winner takes all. Only one person gets the top job; only one woman gets to marry Prince Charming. In nature, there is only one leader of the pack, and for eons, the course of civilization has been changed by bloody battles where the winning side enslaved the losing side. We are programmed to reach for the gold medal, and this extends to our investing lives.

The problem with investments is that it is hard to find the gold-medal fund that will help us achieve our goals. What if we went against our human nature?

Instead of beating ourselves up, trying to achieve the perfect investment, what if we settled for good enough investing?

Decades after I watched the Olympics for the first time, my weekly fitness regime consists of walking Sterling the hound, a yoga class and one gym class. Am I at an Olympic level? No. Is this good enough for maintaining my health and hopefully keeping me fit into old age? More than good enough.

What's your 'good enough' investing strategy? Is it outsourcing to a trusted wealth manager? Is it buying simple passive indexes as Warren Buffett recommends? Is it finding a few reputable fund managers and trusting their discretion to make the right decisions for you? Instead of aiming to be the next Warren Buffett or finding the next Google as an investment, maybe for us mere mortals, a 'good enough' investing strategy makes the most sense.

Use your amazing superpower

Living in the heart of global finance in London, I sometimes find little old me sitting next to the titans of finance. Once, when I was seated next to a woman who had been one of the most senior people at a mega-fund management company for over a decade, our conversation turned to career planning and staying with a firm for a long time.

Taking the opportunity to gain a career advice gem, I asked, 'How do you plan your future at your firm?'

Her reply? 'Given the financial industry, I never assume I'll have my job more than two weeks ahead of time.'

This shocked the Manolos off me. Fear of being demoted or fired was commonplace for a mid-level employee like me, but not for a seemingly all-powerful person who had dozens of famous fund managers under their command. It made me truly realize that everyone in the investment management business is always being measured and judged. Even for the most senior people, the horizon is just a few weeks away.

Quarterly goals dominate every industry, but in fund management, they are make or break. Investors will quickly leave a fund that appears to be dipping downwards. With a few exceptions, professional investors are stuck making decisions for the short term rather than the long term, and they end up making the best short-term decision for their careers rather than for you.

Let's turn the spotlight back to you. Most people investing money don't really need it back quickly. For example, I'm hoping my kids will go to college, and I'm hoping I'll be able to pay for it. They are still watching cartoons, so I've got years before I need to access my investments to pay for this. Perhaps you're in your fifties and thinking about money for your old age. You probably have another ten to twenty years before you'll use the money you are investing today, maybe even longer.

There seems to be a total misalignment of timescales between professional investors and those of us giving them our money. Professional investors are investing our money on a short-term basis, while we need it invested for the long term. Our investing superpower is being able to invest for the long term (at least three to five years), so we need to exercise that superpower. Long-term investing is not a crowded space.

Unfortunately, like Superman, we long-term investors must watch out for our own energy-sapping soul-sucking kryptonite. We have an endless number of choices in investing our money – we can buy and rent houses, invest in mutual funds (almost 9,000 to choose from in the U.S.A. alone), invest in China, invest in biotech stocks, buy a goat farm in Italy. The list is endless, and it can lead to analysis paralysis. I fall victim to this myself, swimming around in circles, unsure what to do.

Invest for the long term and don't be constrained by the quarterly results demanded by many investing professionals. When you find yourself cursing the financial industry and its boom and bust cycles, remember you have a superpower over even the best professional investors. Your kryptonite is the endless number of investing choices leaving you confused and paralyzed, but remember, you're Super(wo) man. Anytime you find yourself getting stressed out about investing, remember it's the kryptonite, not you.

Here are some good habits that can give you a long-term investing mindset:

Don't follow CNBC or the markets every single day. Yes, the stock market will go up and down many times in your lifetime. None of us knows when or by how much. Unless you're a full-time trader, think of your investing as a long-term game. Personally, I'm careful about financial news. I try to care about where a price will be in three years or five years, not where it will be tomorrow.

Read analytical pieces rather than real-time news reports. *The Economist* is perfect as it gives you the week's latest news, looking back on it rather than following events as they unfold.

Follow the writing of long-horizon value investors as they explain the advantages that average investors have over professionals and how to use these advantages to achieve financial success.

The obvious place to add to your knowledge are the annual letters written by Warren Buffett[2] dating back

2   www.berkshirehathaway.com/letters/letters.html

to 1977. Additionally, I would recommend reading Seth Klarman's book *Margin of Safety*. Howard Marks of Oaktree Capital writes a free memo with his insights on the economy.[3] Francisco García Paramés has written the more theoretical *Investing for the Long Term*, and Joel Greenblatt explains value investing basics succinctly in his book *The Little Book that Still Beats the Market*. One of the original value shops, Tweedy, Browne Company L.L.C.[4] host an online value library of research and thought pieces going back for decades. *On Value* by Charles Brandes, *The Dhandho Investor* by Mohnish Pabrai and *The Education of a Value Investor* by Guy Spier should also be part of your essential mini-library to get you started in value investing.

Take the right action

The *Bhagavad Gita* (which translates to the *Song of God*), composed around 500 BC, is a holy book that distills the teachings of Hinduism. One of the most popular *shlokas* (couplets of Sanskrit verse) would translate in English to:

You have the right to perform your actions. But you are not entitled to the fruits of the actions.

---

3   www.oaktreecapital.com/insights/howard-marks-memos
4   www.tweedy.com/research/index.php

Our brains haven't changed much in the 2,500 years since this shloka was written. The lesson I take from this is that you must act in life, without attaching yourself to the result. Not acting or deciding is not the right way. Investing is exactly like this. You invest something without knowing what the yield might be in the future – it may go up or down. But not acting is deadly with inflation and opportunity costs.

Despite the rise of A.I. and terabytes of investing information, we must still interpret, act and decide on our investments. Here are some suggestions to help you overcome inaction.

Forecast free

Educate yourself in forecast-free investment thinking. The financial news is constantly trying to predict the future of a certain company or country's economy. We don't know how things are going to pan out in the world economy in the long term, which industries and regions will boom, and which ones might wither away. Warren Buffett's partner Charlie Munger only reads history books. Ray Dalio, one of the most powerful investors of today, is also a fan of history books. History teaches us that the world gets better and better. We can never predict how or from where ideas come, but ideas and people have prevailed over decades, and as a human race, we are healthier and wealthier than at any other time in history.

If you currently spend half an hour a day tracking stocks and reading the financial news, why not use half that time, fifteen minutes a day, reading a history book to help your mind think more long term. Your portfolio and future self will thank you for it.

Do what you enjoy

Another strategy is to outsource appropriately. Successful investors have an army of helpers. They might, for example, buy sector research or talk to accountants, then do certain things for themselves. Some have complicated accounts but maintain all their own books. Some think writing an investing blog would be the scariest thing in the world to do, but I find it rather fun. You can't do it all, so strategically outsourcing areas of investing helps you leverage the skills and strengths of others. But sometimes it's difficult to decide what to outsource and what to do yourself.

Here's a little graph I've made up where the Y (vertical) axis relates to how much enjoyment you take from performing certain tasks and the X (horizontal) axis is how competent you are at said task. Life is short, so aim to be working in the top right-hand quadrant where you have high competence and high enjoyment.

	Low Competence	High Competence
High Enjoyment	Learning Opportunity (Eg. following tech unicorns)	Do it Yourself (Eg. stock picking)
Low Enjoyment	Outsource completely (Eg. filing taxes)	Mostly Outsource (Eg. picking bond funds)

- Low enjoyment + low competence (like me and taxes) = definitely outsource it

- Low enjoyment + high competence = probably outsource it

- High enjoyment + low competence = keep learning

- High enjoyment + high competence = definitely do it yourself

Here are some items in your investing life you might place in your own graphs:

- Accounting and taxes

- Financial planning

- Fund picking

- Bond picking
- Real estate
- Angel investing
- Tech stocks
- Stock picking
- Risk management
- Asset allocation

The power of no

The most important word in an investor's vocabulary is 'no' – don't invest in it, don't think about it, don't tell other people it's on your list of things to invest in, just *no*. A big source of stress in making investing decisions is wasting time and energy on areas you don't have expertise in, but feel you should investigate.

Most people who have money to invest are inundated with opportunities: real estate, startups, friends' restaurants, the latest hedge fund, a timeshare in Bora Bora... the list goes on. And many people I speak to are overwhelmed by these choices. They feel they should take a look if the proposal is from a friend or in a hot new area (like cryptocurrency).

I say what about making a 'no list' – areas of investing that don't interest you or align with your goals? Anytime you spy something in your inbox that tempts you, look at your no list. It's easy. Then if it doesn't align with your goals, you can let the other person know that their offering is not within your circle of competence. It's not personal; it's just an area you don't invest in.

When in doubt, it's OK to channel your inner Nancy Reagan and 'Just say no'.

Cultivate an abundance mindset

One hundred and fifty years ago, the ruler of England was the most powerful person on the planet. But they didn't have flushing toilets. They didn't have penicillin. They didn't have antibiotics or vaccinations. Queen Victoria could summon courtiers, horses and legions of soldiers, but a toothache could have caused her a world of pain, and possibly serious infection and death. Nowadays, a lowly office worker who is barely on the economic food chain drives home in a car that can go at 90 miles per hour. If they get a toothache, a quick visit to the dentist, pain meds and infection control will mean they're only likely to need a day's recovery time – barely a blip in the life of most ordinary people. Since the age of Queen Victoria, give or take a few meteors landing on the earth, nothing has changed the net mass of the planet. It's all human ingenuity that has given us antibiotics, vaccines and painkillers, and created the iPhone and the temperature-controlled buildings we live in with plumbing, electricity and WiFi.

If you think of the world getting better and better in the long term, that helps to counteract the daily ups and downs of the market. In the last 150 years, we have suffered World War I, World War II, several financial crises, the seventies oil crash, India being under socialism, Russia under communism, and a litany of disasters. Even though these horrible things happened, our collective lives have improved globally. We have running water, electricity, smartphones. We no longer worry about diseases such as polio or A.I.D.S.. Our children, for the most part, survive into adulthood. We can get on a plane and be at an exotic beach on the other side of the world in a few hours. We have fresh fruit and vegetables sourced from around the world. People are being pulled out of poverty at an amazing rate.

Let's bring that mindset to looking at investing. Most news commentators focus on the negative things. Fear makes easy headlines. But during the 2008 financial crisis when the banks became untouchable, Warren Buffett waded into a deal to purchase a slice of Goldman Sachs (whose share price had plunged). Something inside him gave him the confidence to stomach the uncertainty, and he made a huge profit as the economy returned to normal.

But few of us stop to ask why people like Warren Buffett can take the same information that's available to the rest of us and use it to invest so wisely. The companies they invest in publish the same reports we can all access.

> You just have to sit back and let American industry do its job for you.
> — Warren Buffet

This is what Buffett said in a recent rant. Let time and market forces do the work for you. You can label it Buffett's attitude, his mindset, his philosophy. I like to call it the abundance mindset – a belief in acting as if the economy is going to keep growing over long periods, just like the human condition is getting better and better.

Our economy has expanded over hundreds of years. There are more and more goods and services coming onto the market, which means if you invest in the long game, your investments will grow over time.

To have an abundance mindset is to believe in two things:

1. We will figure it out. As a human species, we adapt and evolve. Through technology, improved efficiency and our ability to collaborate and communicate in groups, we can increase trade and goods and services, which results in growing assets for everyone.

2. The economy is growing. With the human population expanding, becoming wealthier and needing more and more expensive shoes and cell phones, the economy will keep growing.

If you believe that technology and human ingenuity will keep us growing, and the economy will grow as a result, then you have an abundance mindset. The rest is just creative destruction. Businesses that seemed robust in the past, like General Motors and I.B.M., are struggling now. Google and Apple, who seem so solid now, may be struggling in twenty years. But if you bet on the economy as an expanding entity, you will grow your assets. Despite climate change and populism, the human race will overcome many uncertainties, just as it has overcome world wars, failed communist states, bubonic plague and famines.

B.B.C. statistics say that having $750,000 in assets puts you among the top 1% richest people in the world. The people most likely to adapt to and harness climate change are the richest 1% of humanity. Instead of feeling sorry for the world, I think about how I can leverage my education and access to financial and social resources to make the world work well – more abundantly for more people.

An abundance mindset forces you to constantly think that everything is working out for our species and planet. It is critical for investors. It's too scary to invest money or leave your safe zone and learn about other areas of investing if you have a poverty mindset.

Leverage automation and new technologies

In 2003, when I first landed in London to attend graduate school, I had to use a little paper book called the *London A to Z* – a book of maps. I would open it up when I got out of the Tube stop and use it to navigate the snarled warren of streets. Or I would have to catch a ride in a black cab. Black cab drivers must know every street in London (yes, every street) to get their driving credentials. It's called The Knowledge. Sometimes I would just get in the black cab because I had no idea where I was going. I didn't trust myself. Back then, getting around London was either time consuming or expensive.

Fast forward to today, and I use Google Maps, which is essentially free for me because it's an app on my phone, to get around. I can drive anywhere in London; I just put the postcode into my phone, get in the car and go. Black cab rides are a rare occurrence for me; I'm usually in an Uber, which I can call up on my phone. The ease of getting around London has gone up and the costs have gone down.

We've had an increase in computer technology and an increase in transport data, and an increase in the way computer technology can deal with data. And we have web services. Technology has made life more efficient. Shopping, transport and travel booking have all moved online. Automation, that wonderful by-product of computers and technology, gives us much greater control.

But what of investing? Most of us are still investing like it's 1999. Investing has not been left behind by technological changes; rather, consumers have been reluctant to experiment, and entrenched players haven't made things easy.

A popular new technology called Robo Advice is a digital wealth manager that asks you questions and provides you with an automated portfolio. Essentially, it asks the same formulaic questions an average wealth manager would ask you and provides you with similar advice. This is what's called passive investing where you can buy themes you think will do well, such as automation, environmental companies, or companies that will benefit from the aging population.

A few years ago, to invest in exotic products like hedge funds, you would have to be a multimillion-aire. Hedge funds usually required a minimum of $100,000 to invest in them, more like a million if they are established. There's no way most people could get in. Now exchange-traded funds (E.F.T.s) copy hedge funds, but you only need $50–$100 to start investing in these products. (By the way, I'm not advocating you do that unless you know what you're doing.)

The dawn of the internet has touched off a revolution in transmitting data. Information that was esoteric and hard to access has become low or no cost to ordinary investors like you and me in the last three to four years. The democratization of information is changing things quickly. We can access thousands of pages of information on any given company almost instantly on our WIFI-enabled devices.

D.I.Y. or outsourcing?

> You need to fill your mind with various competing thoughts and decide which make sense. Then you have to jump in the water – take a small amount of money and do it yourself.
> — Warren Buffett

Imagine for a second that you could hire the perfect person to help you full time with your investments. This person would be completely dedicated to making the right decisions for your wealth. They'd be an investing expert with experience from top-notch institutions. But you'd have to pay them around $150K a year, hire office space for them to work in and supply them with access to the right data feeds and industry conferences. Chucking in some taxes, this would cost you around $300K a year. And I'm being conservative here.

If you hire a financial advisor or a wealth manager, you'll pay fees of around 1% of the amount you give them to manage. This number will be higher in some cases, lower in others, but let's assume 1% to be easy on ourselves. You're a smart person and I'm sure you have guessed where I'm going with this. At a 1% fee, you need $30 million with a wealth manager to have a full-time person dedicated to your financial wellbeing.

If you have $1 million invested with a financial advisor, they make $10K from you a year. That covers maybe half the office Christmas party. You're not exactly going to be the biggest priority.

The reason so many people go down the family office route or invest themselves is that they want a 'kill button': some way of stopping investments they don't want, as well as having control over the process, especially fees. The problem with D.I.Y. or a family office is not only the time and effort involved, but also whether you are choosing the right strategy or employee. The downside of the wealth management and private bank model is that even though there is a lot of consultation and education at the beginning of the process, you have little control over your money once you've handed it over.

Here are my suggestions:

- Go slow, don't rush the decisions.

- Rule of three – speak to at least three advisors before you decide on hiring any professional outsider.

- Do something yourself. There is nothing like diving into an investing area personally. You learn what's happening, get more comfortable with the area, etc.

- Ask lots of questions, especially about fees and how the advisor managed the latest big downturn. Don't go with a manager who is arrogant and overconfident.

- My all-time favorite question is, 'Can I get that in writing?' If the manager promises to sell before a market crash or get you a certain level of return, get it in writing. If they'll do this, great; otherwise, run.

- My second favorite question is to ask how they managed the 2008 crisis. Everyone in the financial world on the floor in September 2008 was in shock. Some people got back up quicker than others, but don't believe someone who rewrites history. If they claim they sailed through that period emotionally and financially unscathed, raise your eyebrows.

- Read Charlotte Beyer's excellent book *Wealth Management Unwrapped*, which lists several questions to ask potential wealth managers.

I often see clients and people who attend my seminars torn between D.I.Y. investing and outsourcing to a wealth manager. My solution is: why not do both? Putting yourself at the center of decision making, whether you choose to outsource, D.I.Y. or a combination, is the essential step to becoming a confident investor.

Further steps

- Do you have a notebook or online tool to keep track of your investment opportunities and decisions?

- What are three new tech investing resources you could explore, or get a trial subscription to?

- Book suggestion: Peter Lynch's classic *One Up on Wall Street: How to Use What You Already Know to Make Money in The Market.*

- Book suggestion: Charlotte Beyer, *Wealth Management Unwrapped: Unwrap What You Need to Know and Enjoy the Present.*

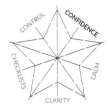

5

Confidence – Learning From The Best

Your investor's edge is not something you get from Wall Street experts. It's something you already have.
— Peter Lynch

How would God invest?

If God happened to work in investment management, have you ever wondered what kind of investor He would be? Firstly, He would have a lot of money to invest, billions and billions. Second, He would have a long holding period (eternity), so He could invest in things that take time to give a good return, and not worry about small ups and downs. Lastly, using His godly powers, He would be able to summon the best investments on earth managed by the cleverest and most competent investment managers.

The nearest we can come to a God of Investing is, of course, Warren Buffet, who has averaged a return of 19.4% for over fifty years. Warren Buffet is a value investor, which means he buys low and sells high. But what about other God-like investors? They are the super-smart university endowments – Yale, Stanford, Harvard, Massachusetts Institute of Technology (M.I.T.), etc. Many of the prestigious private universities have large endowments running into the billions. Since the plan is to keep the university open forever and the endowment is there to fund that, the managers of these endowments have a long-term outlook and can think of a holding period of forever. And due to the universities' prestige and clout, they can get the best investment managers in the world.

How's that for some Zeus-like thunderbolts? Warren Buffett, and the investment managers at Yale, Stanford and M.I.T.? How do they think about investing? We'll turn to the most famous investment manager of all, Warren Buffett, in a while. Then we'll turn to the super-smart geeks. But first, let's go off the wall and take a look at… Santa's elves?

Santa's elves

Most people have heard of value investing, which is basically the principle of buying low and selling high. Simple. But it's more complicated than that.

A value investor needs to buy quality investments that are temporarily low in price while avoiding value traps, which are investments that are low in price for a reason. In other words, they are going to stay low. The most critical value-investing trait is to be patient for the long term, at least three to five years.

Although value investing is mostly used in the context of stocks, I encourage you to apply it to bonds, real estate and every other investment category. In my own life, I use value investing as a mental model for approaching anything investing related, rather than just a tool for stock pickers. There are hundreds of books about value investing. It is the way the greatest and longest-standing investors have ethically made their money.

Elf Val and Elf Norm

I will now illustrate how value investing works with a simple story about two of Santa's elves in the post-Christmas period. The first elf is called Elf Valerie, who employs a value-based approach towards her toy business. We'll call her Elf Val for short. The second elf is called Elf Norman, who uses a normal investing approach. Let's call him Elf Norm.

It's January 1, the first day of the year. Elf Val and Elf Norm are recovering from the Christmas festivities. The other elves are in a bad mood as they go back to work. Everyone wants to forget about the hell of the Christmas toy season and move on.

Elf Val and Elf Norm have each been handed $100 as their Christmas bonus. Elf Val spots boxes of toys for sale. They won't be much use until next Christmas, so the other elves are selling them at giveaway prices. She picks up a box of cheery Christmas wrapping paper and ribbons, and a tub of Lego sets.

It's -50 degrees at the North Pole, so one of the other elves hands her a case of sunscreen for a penny. She notices the mini railway lines and wagons that the elves use to load toys onto the reindeer sleds are all broken and falling apart. No one needs them anymore. She hears the railway system is up for sale as it's useless now that Christmas is over.

Elf Val spends her entire $100 buying discarded post-Christmas sale stuff. Everything is massively discounted, and the other elves laugh as they hand over their unwanted goods to Elf Val.

Elf Norm is vaguely aware of Elf Val, but he's nursing his New Year's Eve hangover. February is around the corner and he's going to buy some chocolates and roses to sell on Valentine's Day. After all, elves are true romantics.

The year goes well for Elf Norm. He is an industrious guy. After making a bit of money on the Valentine's

Day chocs, he buys and then sells green beer for St. Patrick's Day and manages not to drink his inventory before the festival. Good boy. For Easter, he buys daffodils and chocolate Easter eggs to sell. He hustles hard and is a popular fellow who gets invited to lots of elf investor parties as he is always around.

By May, the other elves have mostly forgotten about Elf Val. No summer party invitations come her way. A balmy spring turns into a blisteringly hot summer, and on June 21, the temperature is nearing 100 degrees.

It's the Summer Solstice Elf Fair, when all the elves have a daylong picnic in the sunshine with cucumber sandwiches, elderflower jam cake and elfin cordial. The elf mommies are worried about their elfin babies in the sun. Where is the sunscreen? It's suddenly in high demand, and every family wants a bottle so that they can enjoy the festivities without elf-burn. Elf Val shows up and sells everyone a bottle of sunscreen for $1, which is a reasonable price for her customers, but a huge profit for Elf Val who only paid a few pennies for the case.

Elf Norm sees Elf Val making a tidy profit but thinks it's a fluke. It's an active summer for Elf Norm. Burnout busy. He buys and sells coal for elf barbeques. He makes quite a bit on elfin swimsuits. He launches an ice cream business with much of his profits, thinking how much his elf friends love ice cream. Other elves, seeing his success, also start patrolling the parks selling ice creams, and Elf Norm is forced to drop his prices.

The weather cools and summer turns to autumn. Elf Norm is still fashionable and going to elf parties, but he's getting a bit tired from all the buying and selling, and mostly all the decision making. Elf Val seems to have faded away; she's not even posting her status on Elf Book.

Halloween approaches. There is a sharp nip in the air. The other elves are now thinking of the Christmas season. Boy, will they need a lot of help. Elf Norm sorts out some Halloween candy for his shop and some Christmas baubles to sell over the festive period. He's constantly worried about the post-Christmas crash, so he's not so enthusiastic about taking on too much, just in case.

Elf Val finally makes a reappearance, all glammed up with a feathery festive scarf. First, she offers the other elves rent of her elf railway to bring their presents to Santa's sleigh. At first, there is just a bit of interest, but as the elves get busier and busier, they are paying her higher and higher rent to use her railway. On Christmas Eve there is a queue that stretches around the Christmas tree as the elves line up to transport their toys speedily.

Lego is a classic toy that generations of children have enjoyed and is always in demand at Christmas. A large toy store can't source enough Lego sets and pays Elf Val double what she paid for them nearly a year ago. Elf Val has made a mistake, though. The cheery wrapping paper and ribbons aren't really in fashion this year. A few dorky elves do help themselves at a steep discount, but the cool girl elves won't be seen dead with their presents wrapped in last year's colors.

It is now December 31, a year since we first met our elfin friends. There is a large Elfin New Year's Eve party that everyone is invited to. Even Elf Val, who doesn't seem so un-cool anymore.

Elf Val and Elf Norm hold hands as the elfball gets ready to drop. I should have mentioned that somewhere towards Christmas, Elf Norm started finding Elf Val quite interesting and they're good friends now.

Elf Norm thinks back on his year. He started at $100. He bought and sold on Valentine's Day, St Patrick's Day, Easter, Mother's Day, Elfin Day, etc. etc., made a bit of profit each time and is up overall. But when he calculates the loss he made on his ice cream business, he is ending the year with $135. Not bad, he thinks, until he factors in the fees for buying and selling all those goods. About a $1 a pop. That sets him back $20, and he reaches midnight at $115. Still not bad, he thinks. That's about what the average elf makes in the market each year anyway. It was hard work, though, and he thinks when he receives this year's bonus from Santa, he might just put it under his mattress and have an easy year ahead.

Although Elf Val admires Elf Norm for his entrepreneurial spirit and clever ideas, she thinks she has probably done better than him. She chalks up her numbers. She bought four things, so lost $4 on trading costs. She took a large hit of $25 on her wrapping paper misadventure, but the Lego sets sold for double their original price, so she made up for that quite nicely. She made a ridiculous return on the sunscreen by buying when there was no sun; we're at the North Pole, remember. But where she really won was the elf railroad. There was no other railroad the elves could use, and they had to use hers for their toy transport.

She adds up her numbers and the total comes to $125. Not bad, thinks Elf Val. Then Santa comes up to her. He would like his railway back so he can set the price and control the naughtier elves next year. He offers Elf Val $25 a year for ten years for rights to her railroad.

Elf Val takes the deal and closes the year at $150, 50% more than she started with. She can also look forward to a future flow of elf cash from Santa's railroad rent. She spent a long time being unloved and made a few mistakes. Overall, though, she expended very little of her energy and is ready to make a killing the next year.

Elf Norm looks at what is going to go up in the short term and buys and sells accordingly. This is what most asset managers do. It's not their fault; their clients expect them to keep doing work and coming up with ideas. They want constant reports and follow Elf Norm like hawks. Ooh, elves and hawks? Not a good mix. Shouldn't have mentioned that as this isn't a murder thriller.

Elf Val is a true value investor. She paid a low price for some items and a reasonable price for others. She bought just a few quality things and held them for a long time. In particular, her railroad had a moat – it was the only one around. She respected the cycle of the year, knowing things would swing her way again eventually, even though she had to endure being irrelevant for a long time.

Let's take Elf Val's Lego sets, which are a bit like housing and other real estate. When real estate was beaten down in 2008/2009 in the United States, professional long-term value money managers moved in. They studied the housing market and realized that the U.S. housing stock would have to keep going up to match the needs of a growing population – couples having babies, young adults leaving home, immigration, etc. They knew that although mortgage lending was nearly frozen, it would recover, and with it the house prices across most of the United States. They swept in with their analysts and brought up houses at low prices, held onto them for a few years, and then sold them on for huge profits as the housing markets recovered around the country.

They made their money by:

1. Buying when no one else would
2. Being able to find the cash from trusting investors to buy when prices were low
3. Buying when the prices were falling
4. Holding on for years with confidence that the markets would recover

The wrapping paper and ribbons that didn't sell well for Elf Val in the end were a value trap. She bought the stock thinking that getting it at a dirt-cheap price after Christmas, she could sit on it for a year, and then when Christmas wrapping paper was needed again, she could flog it for a tidy profit. Unfortunately, the fashion changed.

It reminds me of the time I bought shares in a luxury handbag company. The shares had been languishing for years, but the management had invested heavily in a turnaround, rebranding and celebrity campaign. This convinced me to buy, but the great uplift I had hoped for never came. The company's accessories did become fairly popular again but didn't sell in the volumes I needed.

Warren Buffett likes railways. They are still a cheap form of transport for bulk goods, even when compared to trucking. Because it's so hard to build a railway, the railway owner essentially has a monopoly over the sections of line they own.

Buffett's holding entity, Berkshire Hathaway, took a stake in Burlington Northern Santa Fe Corp (B.N.S.F.) in 2006. When the price plunged in the 2008 financial crisis, he then bought the entire railroad in 2010. He spent over 26 billion dollars to acquire the part of B.N.S.F. that Berkshire didn't already own.

Since then he has reaped the rewards of being a railroad titan with stakes in other U.S. railways. The B.N.S.F. track network puts it among the best situated of its peers to meet shipping demand where oil production has boomed.

The four ways to make money

In his book *The Most Important Thing*, Howard Marks sets out the four ways to make money via value investing. Marks is a super-successful value investor who manages over $100 billion at Oaktree Capital Management (yes, that is billion with a 'b').

1. Rise in value

You make money waiting for an investment to rise in value. For example, Apple is a famous and expensive company, but you think it is innovative and will create more value, so you hope to buy now and sell at a higher price in a few years. Then a friend comes to you with a hot new biotech investing idea. It's going to change the world. Your $10K investment could turn into $100 million. The problem, of course, is knowing which investments to put your money into. You have to hope you have better analytical skills than other players in the market.

2. Debt/leverage

You borrow money and hope the price of your investment goes up. For example, you buy a house for $100,000, putting down $20,000 and borrowing $80,000. The house goes up in value and you sell for $130,000. You pay the bank $90,000 ($80,000 loan plus $10,000 in interest). You now have $40,000 instead of $20,000. Congratulations – you've doubled your money. Unless, of course, the house price goes down.

3. Selling for more than it's worth

You sit around, hoping someone will pay you more for something than it is worth, like your used car or shares of a company that may look rosy in the papers, but since you buy a lot of its products, you know it is doomed. Great scenario, but unrealistic, and it's probably illegal to engineer this situation.

4. Paying less than its value

Buying something for less than its value and waiting for its market value to catch up, according to Howard Marks, is the most reliable way to invest money. This is what the longest standing investors do.

Value investors love falling markets. We're like the vultures of the investing world. It's a bit of an inverse of the Black Friday shopping sale scenario. In retail, if toasters plunge in price, people line up around the block and try to kill each other to get hold of those discounted toasters. In the stock market, when prices fall, people rush out the door in a near stampede. If you can keep your calm and remember that the market won't stay down forever, buy things that are being hammered down undeservedly and keep investing for the long term. Don't worry about the day to day unless you are a professional money manager. Simple principles, but they're not so easy to follow.

The strategies of value investing

Within value investing, there are several distinct strategies that investors spend a lifetime exploring. The book I like best when it comes to outlining value-investing approaches is *The Manual of Ideas: The Proven Framework for Finding the Best Value Investments* by John Mihaljevic. This book has been invaluable to me. To keep things super simple, I've outlined the top five strategies from the book that are easiest for individual investors to implement. I realize I'm glossing over what intelligent investors spend a lifetime becoming good at, so as a small compensation, I've listed my favorite books on the subject at the end of the chapter.

Good and cheap. Look for stocks that are of good quality, but perhaps temporarily low in price. This could be due to an economic downturn, a faulty product launch or a C.E.O. scandal.

Jockey stocks. Pick companies that have exceptional leaders (jockeys) who can steer the company (the horse) successfully over many years. Apple under Steve Jobs and Berkshire Hathaway under Warren Buffett are two of many examples.

Copycat. The buying and selling activities of the larger funds are reported to regulators. Although the information is delayed by weeks, for long-term investors, following the picks of the superstar investors is a good bet.

Small companies. Research has shown that smaller companies outperform larger ones over time. As large investors need to make large investments to deploy their capital, they often can't invest in smaller companies, so the ups and downs of these small companies are good hunting grounds for the savvy individual investor.

Special situations that may result in a future increase in value, such as spinoffs, bankruptcy, recapitalizations, mergers, restructuring, risk arbitrage and rights offerings.

The super smart

Let's turn back to the other God-like investors now, the university endowments of Stanford, M.I.T. and Yale with billions to invest, an investment period of eternity and access to the best talent. Yale started the trend of well-managed university endowments a few decades ago, mainly through the leadership of an alum named David Swensen, and has posted market-beating returns since he took over under what the envious rest of us call The Yale Model. Stanford and M.I.T., and other universities started copying this model and hiring Swensen's protégés. They've since posted double-digit returns over decades.

The secret is in what they invest in. They spread their bets in several different areas, beyond just stocks and bonds, and bet heavily on private investments with a value-investing approach. They also invest in natural resources (oil and gas, metals, minerals, forests) as well as lots of real estate.

Most asset managers have quarterly targets and clients to hold onto. They are trying to make their money for their clients in the next quarter, otherwise their clients will leave them. Stanford and Yale don't care because it's their own money. Luckily for us investors, the university's investment endowments[5] need to remain publicly accountable to their students and alumni and therefore annually provide their asset allocation and general investing trends that we can then peruse. I encourage you to look at how the successful university endowments think about investing and how they allocate and rebalance their capital.

The universities invest differently from each other, but they all invest in more than just plain stocks and bonds.

The endowment investment manager, unlike a regular asset manager, essentially must answer the same questions you and I consider for our personal portfolios:

- How much do we outsource to managers, how much do we trust ourselves to invest internally?

---

5   Stanford endowment: https://smc.stanford.edu/; M.I.T. endowment: https://mitimco.org/; Yale endowment: http://investments.yale.edu/

- Is there any homegrown advantage we can rely on to manage part of our portfolio?

- How do we decide between investing domestically and in foreign stocks?

- What part of our portfolio do we invest in safer bets like cash and bonds?

- Are hedge fund (absolute return) and private equity fees worth it?

Keep in mind that university investments are tax exempt and are in addition to the endowments sitting on large tracts of land, historical buildings and intellectual property such as patents that can cushion the universities' risk taking. You (I'm guessing) and I most definitely don't have those luxuries. But as they're universities, they're there for the public good, you can look at their investment approach and asset allocation on their websites. Alternatively, David Swensen has written a book aimed at non-God-like investors called *Unconventional Success: A Fundamental Approach to Personal Investment* that has been useful to many individual investors.

Copying the big cats

The U.S. Government's Securities and Exchange Commission (S.E.C.) is the nation's regulatory body to ensure that shareholders are informed of major ownership changes in public companies. This is to protect companies from secret takeovers. A fund manager who has over $100 million in assets under management has to file a quarterly report, called the 13F, with the S.E.C. to disclose their latest investment holdings. Onerous for the investment managers, but a peek into their world for the rest of us, the 13F must be filed within forty-five days of the end of a calendar quarter. We can then use it to copy some of the bigger value investors by looking at their filings. True value managers tend to buy and sell shares only occasionally as their outlook is longer term, that is investing, not trading. Their 13Fs therefore are useful to individual investors even if the data is a few months old.

Value investors are slow and steady investors. They tend to hold shares for years. Warren Buffett claims his favorite holding period is 'forever'. By searching for the latest 13F, you can see what equities he has bought or sold. You can see how his allocation in various sectors has changed over time. The S.E.C. website is difficult to navigate, so to look at Buffett's latest bets, I would recommend a website that pulls in all the data from the S.E.C. and puts it into an easy-to-visualize, user-friendly form.

And his bets are worth looking at. The University of Nevada published research that concludes that if you bought Warren Buffett portfolio changes a month after they were publicly available over thirty years, you would average 14.26% a year, beating the S&P 500 Index.[6]

The financial regulators of other countries also require fund managers to publicly disclose large holdings. For example, an investment manager must immediately inform the U.K. regulator, the Financial Conduct Authority (F.C.A.), if they pass the 3% threshold of voting rights of a U.K. listed company, and after that if their stake increases.

But I'm not advising you to rush off and fire your investment manager and start investing yourself. Do you know what percentage of your portfolio to buy of each holding? Do you know when to sell? Do you understand the company you are purchasing and how it fits into your overall portfolio? How will you know when things are going wrong with the investment? Although I would never advocate blindly copying an investment manager, the disclosures of larger fund managers are good places to look for investment ideas.

Long-term investing

Long ago in 1900, tired clerks in various parts of the world typed up the share prices of stocks in their

---

6   Martin, Gerald S. and Puthenpurackal, John, *Imitation is the Sincerest Form of Flattery: Warren Buffett and Berkshire Hathaway* (April 15, 2008). Available at SSRN: https://ssrn.com/abstract=806246

region in ledgers. For decades, their paperwork lay gathering dust until a few intrepid academics started to piece together the historical returns of investments.

Many of us never question our almost automatic assumption that buying shares in public companies is a great way to invest. The theory behind this thinking is that it's best to bet on economic growth. And the best way to access the returns of economic growth is to buy shares in companies that are public and under the scrutiny and stewardship of public agencies, shareholders and accountants.

That's a nice theory, but being a data nerd, I insist on looking at historical investment returns. Is the stock market the best way to invest?

The *Credit Suisse Global Investments Return Yearbook* is brought out at the beginning of each year. This should be called the *London Business School Global Returns Yearbook* as the researchers are Elroy Dimson, Paul Marsh and Mike Staunton, three professors who have been studying historical returns for decades.

The authors go back to 1900 and find that global equities have returned the highest gains in the last 118 years, even higher for U.S. stocks. They have been publishing their findings since 2002. Since 1900, global equities have beaten bonds and bills, outperforming cash (Treasury bills) by 4.3% and bonds by 3.2% a year – a reward for the higher risk associated with investing in stocks. Over the 118 years from 1900 to the end of 2017, the real return on the world index was 5.2% per year for equities and 2.0% per year for bonds.[7]

Sarasin & Partners also produces an annual report of investment classes around the world. The report has been published since 1997 and is called the 'Compendium of Investment'.[8]

Beware of geeks bearing formulas.
– Warren Buffett

Even when an investor seems God-like, wealthy and highly prestigious, things can go wrong. Confidence comes from not only following the investments of the best, but more importantly putting yourself at the center of deciding who you give money to. Understanding what the best and most successful investors do will increase your confidence.

In this chapter, I have given you the briefest of overviews on how the great investors such as Warren Buffett think and the timing of their investments. The Yale Model gives us all some best-in-class principles to follow, but the most important thing for you to do is act. Investigate some of the superstar investors I've mentioned in this chapter to grow your confidence.

---

7   E. Dimson, P. Marsh, M. Staunton, London Business School. *Credit Suisse Global Investment Returns Yearbook* 2018.
8   www.sarasinandpartners.com/global-home/insights/compendium

Further steps

- List three of the most famous investors you can think of. They must still be alive, and preferably not Warren Buffett or any of the investors mentioned in this chapter.

- Go look up their 13F on the S.E.C. website, or the equivalent outside the United States. What are their most recent purchases? Can you see a trend?

- Pick Stanford, M.I.T. or Yale. Just pick one. Download and read the latest report on their investments at www.investments.yale.edu; www.smc.stanford.edu; or www.mitimco.org.

- Did any of the value investing strategies pique your interest? If you would like to investigate further:

  - Good and cheap stocks: *The Little Book that Still Beats the Market* by Joel Greenblatt.

  - Jockey stocks: *The Outsiders: Eight Unconventional C.E.O.s and Their Radically Rational Blueprint for Success* by William N. Thorndike Jr.

  - Special situations: *You Can Be a Stock Market Genius: Uncover the Secret Hiding Places of Stock Market Profits* by Joel Greenblatt.

6

Calm – Playing Mind Games On Yourself

If you can keep your head when all about you are losing theirs...
   — Rudyard Kipling

The born-again chimp

Let's go back to our chimp in the jungle, swinging in the trees and still refusing to put his bananas in the ground for another chimp to investment manage. As we observed earlier, we make good investing decisions from the logical brain or neocortex. For this to happen, the neocortex needs the right data, the requisite amount of time and the confidence to push the button.

To get into investment decision-making mode, the brain needs to be calm. You cannot have strong anxieties or uncertainties messing up the system, so calm down your emotions and your fight or flight response before making logical decisions. This is all theoretical, of course, because it's hard to do without practice. But it *is* possible, and in this chapter I will give you practical tips to help.

Finding religion

In the 'Confidence' chapter, we looked at how God would invest. Let us now turn back to religion for some higher guidance.

The world's great religions, Christianity, Hinduism, Islam and Judaism, have a similar purpose in common. They aim to give their followers a set of rituals and beliefs that guide and calm their minds in both good times and bad. Putting aside the Crusades, the Inquisition, 9/11 and other horrific byproducts of religions, let's look at how some of their core principles can help us be calmer investors.

Forgive yourself

You *always* make a mistake when buying a certain stock. If it does well, you'll kick yourself for not having bought more initially. If it does poorly, you'll kick yourself for having bought it at all. There is no winning.

So many people beat themselves up about a bad investment in the past, or for not putting their money to work sooner. They regret the money they lost or the investments they didn't make. As appropriate for someone who was brought up in the Catholic faith, I'd like us to begin with confession and forgiveness.

Catholic masses begin with an act of penitence, asking for mercy 'in what I have done, and in what I have failed to do'. How perfect for us investors. What if we could forgive ourselves daily and see ourselves as making decisions anew?

Professional investors are good at moving on. They are forced to be. They have teams to keep employed and clients to handle, so they have to cut their losses quickly and get onto the next thing. When you're investing for yourself, your only client is you. It is easy to get bogged down in should haves, could haves and other self-flagellation. What if instead, every day you accept that you have to leave your past investing mistakes behind and go on. The fact you've read this far in the book suggests you are open to changing and learning in investing.

Take a moment to consider your worst investing mistakes. Then forgive yourself. Put them in the past where they belong. It is time now to move on.

Meditation

Hollywood loves to portray all investors as ranting testosterone-driven lunatics. Whether it's *The Wolf of Wall Street* or *Trading Places*, there is a lot of yelling and flapping of arms supposedly going on to make money. But the people who consistently make the most money over long periods for their clients tend to be the opposite – calm, patient and deliberate in their thinking. They spend a lot of time planning, reading and thinking. They might act quickly when an investment opportunity presents itself, but that's because they've done all the research beforehand. And what's the secret sauce some of the world's most famous investors use to calm their minds? Meditation.

Ray Dalio, the founder of the world's largest hedge fund, attributes much of his success to being able to calmly assess the markets to his forty-plus years of meditation practice. Bill Gross of Pacific Investment Management Co., arguably the world's most famous bond expert, regularly practices meditation, and there are several meditation training courses and software to help investors.

Buddhism advocates meditation, a modern form being vipassana. The Hindus continually chant their mantras. The Catholics and Sufis have their rosary beads. All forms of practice take the mind away from its present ego to a calmer plane.

> If it's [meditation] good enough for Ray Dalio, Paul Tudor Jones, Blackrock, Goldman Sachs [all of whom have meditation programs in place for employees] and billions of practitioners worldwide, maybe it's worth considering.
> — J. Voss in the CFA Institute's 'Meditation Guide for Investment Professionals'[9]

I have consistently meditated since I was twenty years old. I had an incredibly hard period in my college years facing exams and needed to get my anxiety levels down, so I enrolled myself in a month-long meditation course. I stuck to it, and my brain changed. Within a month, I was calmer and more focused and able to be objective about my exams. Meditation has since helped me enjoy life and make the right decisions when under pressure.

What is it about meditation that helps with investing? There are three main benefits:

1. Attention levels: meditation increases the total period of attention you can give to a topic

2. Patience: meditation increases your perspective by calming down your thoughts, leading to a more patient view of the world

3. Mood regulation: meditation helps regulate the ups and downs you might react to the market

---

9   http://mmd.cfainstitute.org/courses/MeditationGuide/story_html5.html

with, giving your rational brain the time to make more deliberate decisions

The analogy that I like to use for meditation is combing your hair. In the morning, your hair is a mess from sleeping. You comb it into place, and it helps set you up for the day, ready for anything. In the evening, your hair has been blown about by the wind and is messy again. A few minutes of combing has everything going in the right direction. Meditation does the same for your brain.

Rituals

Scattered attention and haphazard decision making are the hallmarks of the individual investor. Whereas professional investors have desks to be at, bosses to keep happy and endless meetings to check in with, when we are investing for ourselves, there is rarely a consistent cadence.

The ancient religious traditions bring people together in regular rituals. The druids mark the Summer Solstice at Stonehenge. Judaism has its weekly Sabbath. Catholics go to mass on Sundays. Muslims attend the mosque on Fridays. It's a check-in, a reboot and a refresh for the mind.

Another way of saying 'ritualize it' is 'schedule it'. Do you have an annual review of your portfolio scheduled? Do you check in monthly or weekly with the best newsletters and investors? Do you have a rhythm of making investment decisions or automatically investing money?

Schedule – once a month, week, year – investments of your money automatically using apps or direct debit. Next, schedule your time. It doesn't count if you're looking at C.N.B.C. or *The Wall Street Journal* for five minutes a day or twenty seconds once in a while. Schedule time to read and think about investing long term. Blocking off regular time in your diary for reading and thinking about your portfolio, just like you might block off time to exercise, is critical to building up a coherent and calm attitude.

A higher cause

Inheriting or coming into a huge sum of money, selling a company or marrying into wealth can bring about feelings of being undeserving and inadequate. Investing it then becomes slightly problematic because investing is all about creating even greater wealth. When it's all about you, it's sometimes hard to motivate yourself.

I consider myself a conscientious capitalist. I was blessed with a terrific education and inherited active neurological pathways, but I fell into finance accidentally and always felt odd about 'making money'. If that resonates with you, let me assure you I was cured of this the moment I decided to work with clients who wanted to give a large part of their wealth to charity when they're gone. This switched my thinking about getting returns from a game to a moral imperative. Isn't it a higher cause for me to maximize my returns and preserve and grow my capital so that at some point, humankind and the environment can benefit from it?

The better I perform in my work, the calmer I make my clients feel and the larger the pot they will leave decades from now. What if you pledge today, either to yourself or in your will, that you will leave a substantial part of your wealth to charities? The Giving Pledge, for example, gets the wealthiest people in the world to make a moral pledge to give away half or more of their wealth.

Sunday school

> The worst thing you can do is invest in companies you know nothing about. Unfortunately, buying stocks on ignorance is still a popular American pastime.
> — Peter Lynch

The shortest of headline-grabbing summaries is all we generally get of company news. My biggest pet peeve is hearing people talk about share prices based on their opinion of a company's products or services. I like to shop at Target, so should I buy Target's shares? But we can find out more in-depth information. Companies put out annual reports in easy-to-read formats these days. You can obtain the annual performance report,

C.E.O. letter and quarterly earning call from a corporate website with a few clicks on your smartphone.

Reading original texts is another important tenet of world religion. The Torah, the Koran and the Bible are required reading in the daily lives of the faithful. The point of reading religious texts is to get back to what the original religious master might have meant. Whether it's the word of Moses, Jesus, Mohammad or Valmiki, reading what was captured of their intentions helps ground their current disciples and insulates against quackery.

If you're interested in a company, the best way to learn about it is to read, or at least skim through, what the company itself is claiming about its strategic direction, earnings, risks and competition, instead of reading the speculation of financial journalists. Reading the annual report of a well-run, robust company will instantly calm you down. You can see they have millions in revenue coming in and they will either weather the storm or they won't. If you decide they won't, you have come from a place of information rather than speculation. You can then invest from a place of information rather than assumption.

Despite people's obsession with Apple or Facebook, how many of us have more than a superficial idea of how these businesses are run? What were their major acquisitions? Their debt levels? How does their executive compensation stack up against their peers? How many iPhones did Apple sell? Is Microsoft's rate of customer retention rising or falling? Where is Amazon growing fastest?

Annual reports are the mainstay of professional long-term value investors. They are the official and final word on the company, audited and rising above the short-term opinions of newscasters and journalists. But few of us shareholders, unless we have to for professional reasons, make the time to read an annual report of a company that our lives are so vested in.

There are stories about some small-fish investor who called the Enron scandal months before it happened, or who had been warning about Lehman Brothers' troublesome choices long before its downfall. These people weren't magicians; they had just been reading the annual report and accounts. If your life and business are linked to the products and services of a certain company, why not learn about how it functions and what its plans are? An annual report runs into hundreds of pages, but I'm sure you're a smart person. You can be efficient. Pick one company to start with. Set aside one hour. Don't get overwhelmed or intimidated. Read the letter from the C.E.O. and at least a summary of the financials. Ignore as much legalese as possible. It's the quickest way to get away from the noise and the hoopla surrounding companies, and if you already know a lot about a company, I promise you will find yourself enjoying the process.

For example, most people think of Alphabet (Google) and Facebook as technology companies. If you read their reports, you will realize that in reality their revenues come from advertising. It changes how you think about their future if you think of them as advertising giants.

Every talking head on TV should have read at least one of these reports before they go on screen, but I'm willing to bet 95% haven't before transmitting their 'opinion' to millions. Scratch that. Let's take that up to 99%. You will have, so you will create a stronger base to understand the companies you are investing in.

Thou shall not

The markets are on 24/7, and there is always a shiny new company or growth trend to investigate. If people perceive you as an 'investor', you'll face a constant stream of investment requests. Between your laptop, TV screen, smartphone and inbox, investment opportunities will be coming at you like machine-gun fire.

Religion is especially useful when it comes to getting you not to do things. Banned foods and banned behaviors litter religious practice: no pork, beef, alcohol, gambling. For me, the best efficiency practice I've started is to have a 'stop-doing list'. You simply stop doing things that you don't truly enjoy or that don't help your investing goals.

This is my investments stop-doing list:

- Types of investments – I don't look at anything that isn't cash flow generating (no venture, moon rockets or unicorns).

- Geography – I only look at companies in the United States, Northern Europe and India. If there is a presentation on China or South Africa, it's out of bounds. China and South Africa have great investment potential, it's just I don't have enough expertise.

- News – I read *The Economist* weekly and *The Financial Times* and *The Wall Street Journal* daily. I've stopped looking at the business news in other papers. Definitely no stock-market apps on my phone.

- Market surfing – I don't track the markets or individual stocks daily. Never ask me what the F.T.S.E. or S&P 500 are doing. It doesn't make me a better investor to follow daily gyrations.

> You can find good reasons to scuttle your equities in every morning paper and on every broadcast of the nightly news.
> — Peter Lynch

The best way to complement your stop-doing list is to stop worrying about expert opinions on the future. Create a stop-following list. Stop watching reports on interest rates or inflation. Unless you need the information directly for your employment, the unknowns can only increase your anxiety.

Give yourself a break from the investing news this week. Instead of plodding through piles of market data that won't make sense to you an hour later, spend the time creating a stop-doing list. Once you stop doing certain things, it becomes easier to curate your incoming opportunities. This frees you up to concentrate on what you have in a calm manner before you decide what you will do. It also protects you from the excitement of saying yes in the moment.

Investing tactics for dealing with market anxiety

Now that we have had a cheeky look at how world religions can help us stay calm, let's turn to a few more concrete tactics for dealing with market anxiety.

The circle of life

In the introduction, I talked about the concept of the creation-preservation-destruction cycle that companies are in. Three of the best active investors these days are Howard Marks, Ray Dalio and Francisco García Paramés. They all come at investing from different angles, and none are household names, but they have a cult-like status in investor circles.

Coincidentally, all three wrote books on investing in 2018. In no order of favoritism, Howard Marks published *Mastering the Market Cycle: Getting the odds on your side*. The basic premise is understanding economic cycles. Ray Dalio published *Big Debt Crises*, which outlines how he thinks about the role of debt in creating predictable economic cycles. Francisco García Paramés, referred to as the Spanish Warren Buffett, brought out the book *Investing for the Long Term*. It relies on the practical Austrian School of Economics and the obvious explanations for market cycles.

Do you see the pattern? These three mega investors have different investment approaches, but they are all thinking deeply about cycles – market cycles; the natural ebb and flow of our economy. How can this concept of comparing individual companies and industries to the cycle of life help us?

Ask yourself before you invest where in the cycle the company is. You don't want to invest in something that is in a death spiral. At the same time, you don't want to overinvest too close to the time of creation (i.e. startups) where ideas can get pulled back into the flames of destruction.

The other thing the cycle can teach us in investing is simple acceptance. It is what it is. When an industry fails, a stock collapses, we see a cycle collapse, and from it will come rebirth and a new creation. We can position our investment portfolio so we stack the decks against destruction and try to take advantage of the forces of creation and preservation.

Also, keep in mind the words from the most famous circle of life from Disney's *The Lion King*:

Hakuna matata. No worries.

Dashboard of doom

If there is one thing in the world I'm excellent at, it's worrying. I am a champion. Best in class. Unbeatable. With the markets, the reptilian part of my brain is at its most scared. Will what has gone up eventually come crashing down?

Yes, it will, and then it'll recover. The problem is we have no idea when, and we could miss out on a lot of investment upside if we stay on the sidelines. Hence the need for all serious investors to have their own 'dashboard of doom'. Boom and doom.

To me, there are two levels of financial Armageddon. The first is a full meltdown zombie apocalypse and the second a monetary crisis, such as the one seen in 2008. For the first, Warren Buffett in his 2016 annual meeting spoke about cyber, nuclear, biological, chemical (C.N.B.C.) as the major catastrophic threats to the economy. In a C.N.B.C. scenario, I'm afraid I can't point you to anything more than the survivalist mecca

Costco, where you can pick up a pallet of tinned food that will last you twenty-five years. Hopefully, you have a nicely lined radiation-proof bunker you can store it in. In the case of more minor scenarios like the 2008 global financial crisis or the 1987 crash, a wise thing to put together is a personal dashboard of doom – some high-level indicators for when the wheels start to come off.

Running around town in London, I'm lucky enough to come across senior management at the big-beast investment firms – people in charge of deploying trillions of dollars. Recently I asked one whether he took investments to cash if he thought there was a high chance of a market crash.

He looked at me like I was an idiot and replied, 'We *are* the market.' If one of the big beasts advises its clients of a market dip, even if senior managers themselves strongly feel there is one imminent, panic would ensue. They make up such a large part of the market and have such a large influence, you would see complete chaos if they made negative statements. Risk managers (to me) tend to be the clearest thinkers about the economy. Instead of getting stuck thinking of just bonds, China or some other narrow market area, they *have* to take the 30,000-foot view. Boom and doom always happen. That seems obvious, but it's brought home by looking at the markets and the economy over the last 200 years. Technology and opportunity cause markets to boom, and then we inevitably have a cooling off and correction period. As painful as these have been for those who've lived through them, the economy without fail has picked back up and gone on its upwards trajectory.

The large asset managers, banks and government agencies like the S.E.C., I.M.F. and Bank of England have their complicated models for predicting down-turns. Buffett uses the indicator market cap/gross domestic product (G.D.P.), U.S. trucking volume and U.S. railway volume as proxies for economic health. The cost of shipping globally, as encapsulated in the Baltic Dry Index (B.D.I.), was watched by predictors of the 2008 Global Financial Crisis (G.F.C.). But what do people like ourselves, who have imperfect infor-mation, do to get a good read on the market? For high-level identifiers, this is the research I'm currently most enthusiastic about including in my layperson's dashboard of doom:

- Northfield Information services (northinfo.com) provides risk tools to some of the largest government-owned funds and asset managers. They host regular webinars where you can learn the latest ways to think about investment risks.

- Now-Casting (now-casting.com), created by a group of academics from London Business School, puts together indicators from world economies to try and make sense of the near future.

- Rosa & Roubini Associates (rosa-roubini-associates.com) was founded by Nouriel Roubini, one of the economists who predicted the U.S. housing downturn of 2008 which earned him the moniker 'Dr Doom'.[10] You can read their weekly column to keep abreast of the latest on how world events are shaping the markets.

Despite writing about doom, it cheers me up that there are folks out there who can read the economy. Thanks to the internet, you too can put together your own personal dashboard of doom to protect what you've made during a boom.

Half and half

I'm lucky I have a huge network in London of different types of financial services and people. If the target interest rates are moving, I have someone I can call. If a Turkish company is doing something weird, there's someone whose opinion I trust to ping.

One thing I used to get stuck on was moving money between the U.S. and the U.K. I'm a citizen of both countries and often need to pay for things in the other country. The foreign exchange rate between the dollar and pound constantly goes up and down. I would worry about making the wrong decision and constantly put off moving money.

---

10 www.nytimes.com/2008/08/17/magazine/17pessimist-t.html

One day I decided to speak to a clever friend of mine who runs the foreign exchange desk of one of the largest vacation companies. When you buy a holiday from a company such as Virgin Holidays or TUI, they take your money from you on the day, but only pay the hotels and other services they book you into when you take the vacation.

Let's say you live in New York, and on a cold January morning, you book a summer holiday in sunny Greece. You pay $1,000 for it in January. In July, your vacation company will owe the hotel in Greece in euros. The euro versus dollar exchange could have moved substantially by then, so the holiday company is taking a currency risk. The euro/dollar might move in their favor. It might move against them. These companies process millions of holiday dollars, so they end up taking substantial risks. They can hedge with complex derivatives, but that is expensive.

I asked my friend how her company dealt with this complex situation. She said, 'Fifty-fifty. We move half now into euros, and we keep the rest in dollars until we need to send it, and then we hope it all works out.'

This is what I've seen time and time again. I've had three jobs working with traders and always marveled at how they made 'gut' decisions about moving eye-watering sums of money around. When making a large bet, they might buy half now and half later.

My friend Louisa, an American, has lived in London for thirty-plus years. For a long time, she postponed bringing her dollars over to the U.K. She didn't know when to bring them over and how much to transfer. Then she attended my seminar on a Saturday, and on Tuesday finally decided to move half the money over because she stopped looking for a perfect solution that didn't exist.

Even the biggest investors, when they get stuck, just put in 50%. It doesn't have to be fifty-fifty, though. You could pick some other proportion. The point is not to be intimidated by trying to make the perfect decision.

Resilient list

We live in precarious times. In investing terms, most of us worry about a big crash in the markets, a roller-coaster plunge downwards.

The best thing to do in a market crash is to turn it into an opportunity, and make sure you have the cash reserved for this. Many clever investors retain cash to take advantage of low prices in a crash, using their cash to buy the undervalued assets that will be the most resilient in coming back.

In a general market crash, investors sell even the most well-run companies. A fund manager who has full faith in a company's management team to weather a crisis still has to sell the stock if the investors in her fund redeem their money and fly to safer havens. Index funds will automatically sell stock as investors divest of them. As a financial crisis stabilizes, investors will come back first to the most defensive investments that will do well in a poor economy.

How do we find the most resilient companies? We can look at companies that recovered fastest after the 2008 crash, such as I.B.M. and General Mills. We can look at sectors such as healthcare and food: goods and services people will continue to buy no matter what the economic climate.

Through the looking glass

Highway 1 winds along the coast of California, hugging cliff edges. It is one of the most dramatic drives in the world and I've enjoyed it many times. The road curves perilously and goes up and down between cliffs. It also zig-zags right and left as the coastline changes. You must be a switched-on and careful driver, always looking out in front of you.

Let's pretend we are driving down Highway 1 from San Francisco to Los Angeles. We have a choice of three instruments to use that could help us navigate the ups and downs – a magnifying glass, a telescope and a pair of binoculars. Which one would be the most useful for our journey?

Magnifying glass

Imagine traveling down Highway 1 constantly looking through a magnifying glass. Driving would be difficult. The highway signs on the street would be nearly illegible; you might miss your exit.

A magnifying glass view of the market might look like this: here's the S&P plunging in the first few hours of trading today... and then it comes up again. Apple stock goes down $5 first thing in the morning, followed by five unverified guesses at why this happened. Then Apple stock goes up in the afternoon and closes at its starting price. Again, many unsubstantiated guesses about why this happened.

Two groups dominate the news on the markets – journalists and traders. They need to know what is happening this minute to every stock in the universe. Traders ask for this information – the banks and investment firms they work for need it. Journalists, along with tweeters and bloggers, feed the need for interpreting the data. Tweets and news stories must get written every single day. That's their job. Trades must be made every day. That's the traders' job.

With a magnifying-glass perspective of the markets, we risk getting a huge dizzy headache. I'd say that's not the right perspective for most of us.

Telescope

The opposite of the magnifying-glass view is the telescopic view. Telescopes are the instruments of astronomers and big thinkers, and economists love the long-term view. They adore predicting the growth rates of China and India. They say climate change will alter the world's cities and make major harbors obsolete. But how useful is this perspective for an individual investing with a five-year timeframe?

Imagine trying to drive down Highway 1 with telescopic vision. A telescope stuck to your eye while you're trying to drive down a curvy coastal road cannot help you at all. You will probably go off a cliff and crash and burn like a scene from a Hollywood movie.

Binoculars

I want to propose that binoculars are the best analogy for looking at investing in a reasonable and sane way. Binoculars are nice and portable – you can pick them up. You use your own eyes and ears, and if you have a goal in the near distance, binoculars are perfect for bringing it closer, but not too close.

Our laptop screens and smartphone stock trackers are the magnifying views of the world. But the minute to minute and even the month to month might not be significant. A long-term telescopic view over twenty-five years is interesting if you are raising children or doing positive things for your health, but corporations cannot plan that far in advance.

A three- to five-year binocular view gives us a better perspective. When you read the financial news about some fund, don't get too anxious and look at daily gyrations. Don't think too much about long-term trends that might go past your lifetime. Use your binoculars.

I shared earlier that I am a champion worrier. Making things like resilient company lists, not looking for perfect decisions, taking a longer-term perspective by ignoring the daily noise of the markets, meditating and aligning my work to charitable causes, I have become a calmer investor. I hope these tactics will help you as well.

We'll now move onto the 'Clarity' chapter, which takes on how to think about allocating your assets.

Further steps

- Do you have a meditation ritual? If not consider downloading the 'Calm' app or the 'Headspace' app on your phone to start one.

- What company matters most to the finances of your family? It could be one that you work for or one you hold many shares in. It could also be one that is geographically close to you and important to the local economy. Find its annual report. Read it.

- Create a list of three types of investing behaviors you are not going to allow in your life anymore. For example, is there an app on your phone that keeps spewing market news at you which you could delete? Are you obsessing about share prices during the day? Unless you're a professional trader, is there a good reason to constantly monitor the markets?

- To understand market cycles, I recommend these two books: Ray Dalio's *Principles for Navigating Big Debt Crises* and Howard Marks' *Mastering the Market Cycle*.

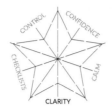

7

Clarity – Making Sense Of Overwhelming Options

Simple can be harder than complex: you have to work hard to get your thinking clean to make it simple. But it's worth it in the end because once you get there, you can move mountains.
  — Steve Jobs

The unicorn cake

My little baby was turning four years old. Now a big girl, she wanted her first big party. There was to be a magic show and disco, and of course, no real party is complete without the *cake*.

Amara is lucky as she has a special friendship with Sophie, the baker. Sophie is the mum of one of her friends and an expert cake maker. With Amara's first ever birthday party coming up, Sophie offered her services.

For months during the school pickup, Sophie and Amara were planning and 'customizing' the cake. First, they came up with a fairy-themed cake. They went through several designs – purple fairies, pink fairies, fairy tree house, fairy garden, etc. A few weeks into planning, Amara went to watch the new *My Little Pony* movie. The fairies were dumped and Amara's strategy shifted. She couldn't decide between a pony cake and a unicorn cake, so Sophie gave her both. Then Amara was specific about the colors she wanted – pink, purple, turquoise *and* lots of sprinkles.

It would be nice if investing worked like this. You start not knowing what you want, keep changing your mind, but still end up with a beautiful portfolio. Unfortunately, the unicorn horn on the cake is a giveaway. Unicorns are imaginary, so that wish is not based in reality.

Wealth managers and investment advisors are a tough breed as they deal with clients:

- Not knowing what they want

- Not understanding how investing works

- Having unrealistic expectations

- Changing their minds

Even if you find yourself a fantastic Sophie-the-baker-like investment advisor, you need to know what you want and understand what's achievable for them to give you accurate guidance. Otherwise, you'll not be getting the best out of them. They're much too polite to tell you to spend time educating yourself, but they can't hold your hand all the time. They leave that to investing oddballs like me.

Some people get upset that their wealth manager is selling them a generic investment product off the shelf. It's not customized. That's because many investors don't understand the basics, so their wealth managers give them whatever is easiest for them to understand and get on with.

> Perhaps the most common investor mistake is chasing returns by overweighting stocks, sectors, asset classes, or strategies that have been successful in recent years.
> — Antti Ilanmen, 'Expected Returns on Major Asset Classes', 2012, CFA Institute

As we look at various asset classes please bear in mind that just because it's worked in the past, is this strategy going to work in the future?

Take a minute to think about what you would like your investing life to look like. Pretty for me, please, with sprinkles on top. Then let's get started with the fourth C in the Superinvestar Framework: Clarity.

HOW THE BEST INVEST

Building blocks

The financial sector works as an engine for the economy. Finance isn't a standalone sector; it powers every other sector by connecting those that have capital with those that need capital.

There are four kinds of wealth:

1. Cash – dollars, sterling, cowrie shells

2. Real assets – houses, buildings, gold in your safety locker, ownership of a uranium mine

3. Equity – shares/stocks (ownership of a slice of a business or corporation)

4. Debt – fixed income/loans (a promise to be paid back for wealth you handed over to a corporation or government body)

Financial services have two major functions. One is to manage transactions for all transfers of wealth. The other is to invest the four types of wealth to generate new goods and services that expand the economy, create jobs and grow industrial sectors where more goods and services are wanted.

An example of a transaction could be going to the cash machine to transfer money from the digital numbers in your bank account to hard cash in your hand. It could mean the process of the bank lending you money to buy your dream house. Investments by the financial sector can range from a fixed-income product which buys and sells the bonds of Chinese industrial companies to a fund that venture capitalists use to develop the next Google or Uber. Every corporation, local authority and government depends on the ability of the bankers to manage the growth of economic goods and services by (a) managing transactions and (b) investing.

How do people have money to invest? There's excess from their salary (savings), it is given to them (inheritance) or they sell other investments.

There are only three fundamental ways to invest.

- Lending a person, business or government money and being paid back for it (bonds, credit markets, fixed income)
- Buying a slice or whole of a business (public or private, small or large)
- Buying goods (art, wine, oil, gold) and hoping that the price goes up due to supply / demand

Although there are only four kinds of wealth and three ways to make money, there are an incalculable number of products and choices in investing.

Ice-cream sundae investing

If you ask ten different investing gurus about their percentage breakdown of asset allocation, you'll get ten different answers. I pulled four investing books off my bookshelf and looked for the ideal asset allocation for a middle-of-the-road investor. Here are the books I looked at:

- *Investing for Dummies* by Eric Tyson. I like this book as it's quick to read and looks at how buying and renting out real estate and owning small businesses (real *and* virtual assets) can be part of your investment plan. He advocates a portfolio of mostly stocks and a quarter of bonds for a mid-thirties middle of the road investor.

- *Investing Demystified: How to Invest Without Speculation and Sleepless Nights* by Lars Kroijer. Lars has managed money and taken punches in the marketplace, and he advocates the use of index trackers. His book is one of the few targeted at U.K. readers. For a medium risk forty-year-old investor he advocates a half and half division between stocks and bonds.

- *Money: Master the Game, 7 Simple Steps to Financial Freedom* by Tony Robbins. Yes, yes, I was highly skeptical that a self-help motivational guru could write an investing book, too. What Tony Robbins has done is distill the investing wisdom of the world's greatest investors (David Swensen, Ray Dalio, Charles Schwab, Paul Tudor Jones, John Bogle) who run billions of dollars successfully. Each guru has their own take as to what normal investors should do. Ray Dalio for example proposes a third in stocks, just over half in bonds and 15% in gold and commodities.

- *The Ivy Portfolio: How to Invest Like the Top Endowments and Avoid Bear Markets* by Mebane T. Faber. This book looks at how Yale and Harvard manage the billions of dollars in their endowments for the long term and teaches the individual investor simple ways of imitating them. The overall conclusion is 40% in stocks, 20% in bonds and 40% in other categories such as real estate and commodities.

Four different books, four different outlooks and asset allocations. No wonder investors are dazed and confused. Even sophisticated wealth managers using advanced software tend to leave out things like people's own homes, other real estate, cash under the mattress, antique watches, etc.

When interviewing wealth managers, I was baffled as to why one wealth manager would want to put me in 34.6% equities, yet on the same day another would want to put me in 42.7% equities. I was bewildered until I learned that asset allocators have relied on spreadsheet models to keep spitting out numbers that take a stab at managing risk and return for an individual investor ever since Harry Markowitz proposed modern portfolio theory in 1952 that everyone rushed to build their models on. With different models and different assumptions going in, no wonder there is a wide range of numbers the models spit out. Always be clear on what assumptions and type of model your wealth manager is using.

My quest for the perfect asset allocation continued as I researched the prestigious endowments. Once again, I found many different approaches. After studying some of the major portfolio engines that drive asset allocations for large investment managers, I finally had to admit defeat and accept that there is no perfect methodology, just general principles. Beware of anyone who sells their model as the perfect one.

David Swensen, the head of the Yale endowment, working with round numbers, says this about his targets for his $26 billion endowment:

> Yale targets a minimum allocation of 30% of the endowment to market-insensitive assets (cash, bonds and absolute return). The university further seeks to limit illiquid assets (venture capital, leveraged buyouts, real estate and natural resources) to 50% of the portfolio.[11]

I came up with an idea for representing asset allocation that has been popular among clients. I call it ice-cream sundae investing. When you build an ice-cream sundae, there are general principles, but no strict rules. You customize it for yourself, leave out stuff you don't want and sprinkle on more of what

---

11 https://news.yale.edu/2018/10/01/investment-return-123-brings-yale-endowment-value-294-billion

you do want, *but* you need to have a base of flavors and good proportions. Also, just as ice cream melts and runs together, sometimes investments can be categorized in more than one way.

When you take your child out for an ice-cream sundae, you do not let them get just a bowl of sprinkles or a tub of decadent chocolate sauce. That wouldn't be very tasty or good for them in the long run. An ice-cream sundae needs a base of ice cream – a big scoop of vanilla bonds, a dollop of chocolate stocks and maybe an additional scoop of strawberry real estate. That's what most people count as their wealth.

But it would be boring just to have ice cream in a bowl, so a lot of people go crazy with the toppings – maybe some private-company chocolate sauce or options-trading sprinkles. If you're brainy with techie things, how about some deep-tech angel investing as the cherry on top? The point is the basic building scoops have to be there and the fun toppings have to be in proportion – no one wants to choke on hedge-fund nuts. At the same time, there isn't a correct answer or a perfect solution. It's up to each person to know what kind of ice-cream sundae they would like for themselves.

Let's build an ice-cream sundae right now. The way you construct it is the way you determine your investing future. I'm not going to get into exact asset allocation here because I don't know who you are or what your future needs are; I'm just going to outline my own sundae. As a careful investor, I like a nice, solid base to my investing ice-cream sundae, so I'm going to choose a banana split with scoops of ice cream, topped with chocolate sauce, sprinkles and a few nuts.

Let's dig in.

The sundae base

Bananas – cash and safe stuff

A lot of financial advice says not to hold cash as it's not earning anything, and inflation eats into your purchasing power every year. The truth is a lot of people want the safety of having cash on hand for emergencies, just in case the stock market crashes. You can always put money in cash equivalents – money market funds and the like – so it's OK to have a cash cushion.

A scoop of chocolate – stocks

Next up is a fat scoop of chocolate ice cream – the perennial favorite. This would be stocks – a suitable mix of diversified shares. A share buys us an equity slice of the company. The fortune of the company as the share price rises and falls, or if the company decides to pay a dividend, is then passed on to us as part owners.

When a company grows large enough, it tends to list itself on a market like the New York Stock Exchange and sell its 'public' shares. Ordinary people like you and me can buy a tiny slice – maybe one billionth of a large company where otherwise we would probably be escorted out of the foyer by security. The World Federation of Exchanges, the global industry body for exchanges and clearing houses, estimates there are over 48,000 listed companies around the world.[12]

Publicly traded companies are required to file accounts and paperwork with the government and comply with local corporate governance. They also usually post several years' worth of accounts and produce annual reports, so are easier to access and less opaque than private companies.

A scoop of vanilla - bonds

A substantial part of your sundae should be plain vanilla bonds – it's not that exciting, but it aims to give a consistent return and holds up all the other flavors.

Large institutions need to take on large projects to keep providing their services. For example, a county or local authority might need to build new housing for the elderly. A large corporation may decide to acquire a smaller company that has new technology it can use. To carry out their plans, governments and corporations

---

12   https://focus.world-exchanges.org/storage/app/media/statistics/
     WFE%20H1%202019%20Market%20Highlights%20press%20re-
     lease%20draft%205%2016.08.2019.pdf

borrow money from investors, who can be as small as you and me or as enormous as a multinational bank.

A bond or a fixed income is a way of lending governments or corporations a little bit of money. In return for the bonds you buy, they promise you a certain amount of interest. As a lender, you will typically be paid back before an equity investor (stockholder). For companies, bonds are a great way to raise capital for projects without giving away ownership of the company, which they would owe equity investors.

A scoop of strawberry – real estate

Next up is another big scoop people like to have – real estate. Let's assign real estate a strawberry flavor.

Real estate is not something that is traditionally on a wealth manager's menu of recommendations, but so many of us like it. Owning a property gives us the feeling of having something tangible we can show for our investment.

Firstly, your house is not an investment. Unless you intend to sell it and downsize or move away when you retire, your house is your home, and you need a place to live. When I talk about real estate, I am *not* talking about the house you live in.

There are two main real-estate categories: residential and commercial. Residential covers houses and apartment buildings. You can own one or many and hope that you will make some income by renting your property out and the house prices appreciating over time. Commercial real estate consists of places of business – shopping malls, offices, laboratories, factories, etc. Businesses can be reliable tenants and this is an area often overlooked by individual investors.

If you're wealthy enough, you can own your own properties, or you can pool together with like-minded friends, but owning real estate is not for the lazy. Even if you have a managing company, at the end of the day, you have a physical asset that is your responsibility. If the washing machine breaks, the bill is coming to you.

Real estate investment trusts (R.E.I.T.s) have gained in popularity. They have expanded in the U.S.A., have recently come to the U.K. markets and are emerging in India. A R.E.I.T. is a company that owns a portfolio of apartments or businesses concentrating in a geographic area or type of building. You buy a share in the real estate, much like you buy a share of stock, and you own a piece of that real estate portfolio. This is a 'virtual' way of investing in property without the headache of owning one, or of owning property in an up-and-coming area even if you don't live there.

Sorbet - index investing

Sorbet is light and refreshing, adding to the ice-cream sundae with a myriad of flavors. Like sorbet is lower on calories than ice cream, index investing is lower on fees than other types of investing. Sorbet can come in the same flavors as ice cream – you can have equity indexes, bond indexes and everything else. All the flavor, but less fat.

Warren Buffett, the most famous investor of our century, is in his eighties. He is still going strong, though, and is one of the best in the world at being an active share/stock/company picker. When he goes, he knows the wealth he is leaving his wife and family will have to be managed properly. Given that he has access to the best investment managers in the world and could park his money with anyone, what has Warren Buffett decided on? His will stipulates that on his death, his money should be put in index funds. It should be managed passively without trying to beat the market.[13]

What is indexing or index tracking? It's buying the whole market and being passive about which companies you select – buying shares in a fund that is automatically invested in a set of companies selected by market capitalization, industry, etc. You don't pay someone to choose outperformers for you; you buy a basket of companies in the space you decide. For example, buying the Vanguard 500 index fund buys you the share performance of the 500 largest companies in the United States. Buying an information technology index fund, if you think that is a sector that

---

13 www.berkshirehathaway.com/letters/2013ltr.pdf

will grow, will buy you a share of the largest tech companies in the world.

What are the advantages? Index funds are lower in cost than other methods of investing since you're not paying for stock-picking 'talent'. Index funds are plug and play – you don't have to be an expert. It's the easiest way to follow the world economy and get to know individual companies without having specific knowledge or expending effort, so it's a good entry point for people who aren't looking to beat the market.

What are the disadvantages? An index fund will never beat the market as you are buying the whole market. If everyone indexed, markets wouldn't function properly. Index funds still go up and down with the market; they don't eliminate market anxiety or stress. You hold good companies and bad. Even if you know a company has fallen on tough times, if it's part of an index you hold, you own that company.

John Bogle, author of *The Little Book of Common Sense Investing*, started the company Vanguard to offer this type of investing to the mass market. It was niche in the last century, but has boomed to the point that in 2019, U.S. investors have as much money in passive strategies as active.[14] Vanguard and Blackrock are now the two largest purveyors of index funds.

---

14 www.institutionalinvestor.com/article/b1fg0jnvbpc536/History-Made-U-S-Passive-AUM-Matches-Active-For-First-Time

Many wealth managers offer their clients advice and platforms to hold index funds as well as actively managed funds. Index investing is supposed to be the 'easy' option, but I strongly disagree with this. If you decide to be a passive investor, you come across a massive problem: you must choose the indexes you want to track. Will the United States do better than China? Will the tech sector index do better than industrials? You need skill and research to decide. For example, logging on to the Blackrock website as an individual U.K. investor gives me over two thousand index and exchange traded fund (E.T.F.) options to choose from. That's *way* more than the number of shoes on display at Selfridges. How on earth is a girl to choose?

Now let's move on to the toppings, everyone's favorite bit. Dear reader, I now must exercise my scolding motherly license on you. Toppings are toppings; they are not the body of the sundae.

The toppings

Chocolate sauce - private companies

We dealt with our scoop of public companies' stocks (chocolate ice cream), so now let's turn to private companies. Public companies have multiple shareholders and their share price is marked to market constantly. Private companies, on the other hand, are not as well scrutinized as they don't have to disclose their accounts to the extent that public companies do. Publicly traded companies are constantly for sale on exchanges, but very few investors will know when a private company is looking for outside investment. This can provide opportunities to find gems, but also puts a higher burden of confidence in making the investment decision on you.

I've divided private companies into three categories:

- Angel investing and venture capital
- Franchises and friends' companies
- Private equity

Angel investing and venture capital

Investing in startup or small privately-owned companies is a favorite pastime of many wealthy people. This type of investing is often called angel investing.

Angel investing targets unknown or startup companies that have a new idea that might turn into a big idea. If you have the right connections, you could find the next big initial public offering (I.P.O.), but angel investing is notoriously difficult to get right as fledgling companies have a million ways to die.

Crowdfunding platforms like Kickstarter and mass-market angel investing like Y Combinator have allowed lots of people to hunt for the next Google or Facebook, but given my experience in Silicon Valley, I know how hard it is to spot the big opportunities. It's a matter of skill and timing. If you have deep experience in a field and an enviable list of contacts and deal flow, this is an exciting life. If you're trying to spot the next Google from your sofa, good luck.

Large pension funds and wealthy families have also started investing in venture-capital funds. Venture-capital funds have a significant deal flow of angel-invested companies that are a bit bigger and more stable than your average startup in terms of business model and direction of growth.

There is a huge amount of fear of missing out (F.O.M.O.) associated with angel investing. It's easy to get caught up in the hype, so the best question to ask yourself is, 'Am I investing an amount I am willing to lose, never to see again?'

Franchises and friends' companies

The second category of private company is a friend's business. Examples could be a restaurant, a chain of McDonald's franchises or a shrimp farm in the Philippines. Investing in a friend's company aims to generate cash flow rather than rely on a sale or I.P.O. like a startup.

Private equity

Private equity (P.E.) funds are the last part of the chocolate sauce. P.E. firms raise money from wealthy individuals and institutional investors like pension funds. They then take over private companies, making them over with changes in strategy or management, and sell them a few years later. P.E. funds are supposed to give outsize returns, but they also charge outsize fees.

Not everyone likes chocolate sauce on their sundae. For those who do, it's decadent and exciting, but remember it's optional. Too much chocolate sauce is rich and can make you ill.

Nuts - hedge funds

Hedge funds are the V.I.P. table at the investment-world nightclub – the table everyone aspires to be on as the champagne magnum is carried over. Why do hedge funds get this rock-star status? Because they promise 'absolute returns'. No matter what the markets do, because hedge funds are hotshots and unconstrained by strict investor mandates, they can hunt for good returns. They do this by employing lots of impressively sophisticated categories of investment, but the best ones turn out to be good, old-fashioned value-investing stock pickers.

Hedge funds have traditionally charged 'two and twenty' – 2% management fees annually and 20% of any performance over a certain threshold (usually 6%). The trouble with investing in hedge funds is that you must be wealthy. The minimum ticket is usually $100,000 to $1 million. But if you can afford it, there are some good hedge funds which are completely worth investing in.

Think of a hedge fund like a Silicon Valley startup or an iPhone app. The first few were good, and now everyone wants to be one. There are over 10,000 hedge funds, but I doubt there are 10,000 superstar investors in the world. The secret to success is picking good managers. This is the world I live and breathe. If, like me, you are comfortable in it, then this could be part of your sundae. But remember this category is the nuts – it's really good if it works, but easy to choke on if you don't know what you're doing.

Sprinkles – shiny, sparkly returns

My girls love sprinkles. Sprinkles are pretty. They're shiny. They only belong on your sundae in moderation, though. Not scoops and scoops, just a pinch or two.

Foreign exchange (forex) derivatives and other speculative trading strategies have splashy advertisements accompanying them, telling us how anyone can make it rich being a day trader. The internet is full of temptations, telling of ways to make money on forex trading, but I'm not sure why people think they can compete with traders in large companies who do this day in, day out and still make losses. And most of these online platforms charge trading fees.

Are you willing to become a day trader full time? It requires much attention, so if you can't answer yes to this question, pass completely. That's why it gets in the sprinkles category – it's sparkly and exciting, but a bowlful of sprinkles does not make for a good dessert.

Smoothies

With the advent of index investing, it has become simple to buy a thematic index. You could add themes you think are going to do well to complement your sundae. Popular ones are sustainability, A.I. and robotics, aging of the population, etc. In investing, we never miss a trick. We have created 'smart beta' indexes that attempt to take the best factors of various investment styles and blend them to create a better index. The index is constructed with companies that are predicted to do well from changes to our society, and the theory is that owning these smoothies should round out our sundae nicely.

Various themes exist in passive investing, too. For example, you can buy sustainable environmental social governance (E.S.G.) funds as well as those that concentrate on A.I., biotech or water companies. There is also the rise of E.T.F.s, which mirror other funds, to consider. For example, foreign investors have a hard time purchasing the shares of Indian companies due to the restrictions on outside investors placed by the Indian government, but it's easy to purchase a variety of India E.T.F. funds that mirror the contents of the funds that hold actual shares in Indian companies. But as of October 2019, E.T.F.s have not been tested in a down market and there are worries about how they will perform if loads of investors rush to the exit in the case of a market fire.

The way I look at these opportunities is to ask myself, 'Does it do what it says on the tin?' Does the fancy index or E.T.F. you're buying truly give you exposure to what you're trying to access? For example, there are several gold E.T.F.s that might seem like a convenient way of holding gold – until you examine the indexes. Some of them are just a list of gold miners. Although they do mine gold, they have their license to operate and extraction capability risks, so I would not deem them a real proxy for physical gold prices.

I examined the fine print of a gold E.T.F. that claimed direct exposure to physical gold, but would only deliver it to you if you owned more than $10 million of the E.T.F. This kind of investing might not give you the doomsday protection that many gold bugs buy the metal for.

I am all for index E.T.F. investing if it gives you access to investment areas that would be difficult for you to get into ordinarily. Just keep in mind that the primary data is being sliced and diced, and then being put in an E.T.F. blender. As the investment area gets more and more crowded, the data will be whirled around faster and faster. The E.T.F. smoothie inside still has the same ingredients, but they are being pulverized – which is fine as long as someone is holding the lid down hard on the blender, but we all know what happens when the lid comes off.

The waiters

Finally, someone must bring you that fabulous ice-cream sundae or make suggestions as to how you build it. I tried to find a good list of definitions for the various types of money management, but couldn't. I have picked up the nuances in terminology by working in the financial markets for many years, and I suspect that's how most of us figure it out. Wikipedia and Investopedia have the longer technical definitions of these terms, but I'm going to break them into basic, uncomplicated language.

Wealth management

This is the broadest definition of investment planning. A wealth manager should help you decide your financial goals and make suggestions about what kind of financial products – equities, bonds, etc. – would be appropriate. They help you decide which portfolio managers and investment managers to entrust with this task. Private banking is wealth management for very wealthy individuals where banks may offer a wide variety of hand holding services. A financial advisor is typically for those with under a million in assets.

Asset, investment and portfolio management

Asset management is a catch-all phrase for formalized investing of all types, be it real estate, stocks, bonds, equities, etc. Investment management refers to picking specific investments. An investment manager might specialize in technology stocks or the Indian market. You pick one or more investment management firms to manage your money once you've planned what assets are right for you.

Portfolio management is the process of deciding which investment mix might work well for certain goals, or what industries and geographies to invest in. A portfolio manager at a large mutual fund will be the decision maker on what types of investments to make, while investment analysts will handle specific investments at a granular level.

To hug and to hold

Whether you use a financial advisor, wealth manager or private banker, the promise they make to you is to hug and to hold your investment until death (or a market crash) do you part. It's not to keep you thoroughly informed or to give you anything other than the company line.

The main goal of most asset managers is not to get fired by their client. They 'hug' the benchmark index, giving you an average market return. If the market falls 20% and your portfolio falls only 15%, most risk-management systems define that as a 'success'.

Your financial advisor/wealth manager/private banker, to a greater or lesser extent based on the level of fees they charge, will hold your hand for the ride. If you're flying from London to San Francisco, an economy flight costs about $1,000. Let's call this the financial advisor equivalent. A business-class ticket is about $4,000, the wealth-manager option. A first-class ticket is about $6,000 that only private bankers can afford. Three different levels of service for the same flight. The economy passenger is squashed in cattle class; the first-class passenger enjoys being wined and dined. If the plane hits turbulence, though, every passenger is on the same ride, plunging downwards.

Don't get mad at your financial services provider if things aren't going as well as you'd like. They are just doing their job and fulfilling their 'to hug and to hold' end of the deal.

Further steps

- How does your wealth manager decide how your assets should be allocated? Is it systematic?

- What geographies are you concentrated in? What one country or one currency are you most invested in?

- What industry do you have most of your assets in?

- What asset class are you in that you think you shouldn't be in?

- Read William Bernstein's *The Intelligent Asset Allocator*.

- Read John Bogle's *The Little Book of Common Sense Investing*.

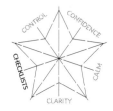

8

Checklists – Essential Qualities Of Any Investment

No wise pilot, no matter how great his talent and experience, fails to use his checklist.
 – Charlie Munger

P.O.W.K.! I was running to the office when I realized that my Oyster card (the prepaid card for the London Tube system) wasn't in my handbag. A few minutes of mad searching yielded no card.

My daughters like to rummage through my handbag or reorganize things for me by 'borrowing' an item. I change handbags now and again, too, and must remember to transfer everything I need. I could survive a nuclear holocaust with the useful bits in my handbag, and to make sure I don't forget the most essential of them, I've learned to use a mental checklist before I step out the door. I call this checklist P.O.W.K.:

- Phone

- Oyster card

- Wallet

- Keys

The power of checklists

The Checklist Manifesto is a book by Atul Gawande that describes why checklists should be mandatory in most professions. He points out that in the early days of flight in the 1940s and 1950s, there were too many plane crashes and too many deaths to make a passenger-carrying airline industry viable. The American military pilots used to have a high mortality rate – pilots with years of experience would forget one little thing and crash. The military investigated the underlying causes and instituted a system of checklists for flights, and the air-crash rate dropped to nearly zero, making the mass-market airline industry possible.

It's surprising to me how many investors don't use checklists. They go by gut feel or invest in things that happen to present themselves. What I have observed from reading the investment processes of the superstar investors is that most are devoted users of thorough checklists before they invest.

In 2008 the value-investor community got a big shock with the stock-market crash. Investments in their portfolio plummeted and never came back up because they had overlooked or ignored an investing principle. Checklists have become popular with professional value investors nowadays, but many are pages and pages long with dozens of headings. If you're a professional investor with the time and knowledge to research a company that deeply this is useful. For a regular investor, a simplified checklist is needed. For my seminars, I have created a generic nine-point Superinvestar Checklist that many participants have found useful.

THE SUPERINVESTAR CHECKLIST

Before making any investment, you need to think about:

- Effort and monitoring
- Lockup and liquidity
- Diversification
- Floor
- Price
- Fees
- F.O.M.O.
- Taxes
- Long-term return

I'll now go through each point on the Superinvestar Checklist in detail using three hypothetical investments as examples of how we might put $1 million to work. This is an illustrative exercise, and no investment will check all the boxes. There is no such thing as a perfect investment.

First up is a friend's hot and sexy Silicon Valley startup. Your friend is a super-smart person and has launched a swish new A.I.-based technology for hospitals. Venture capitalists have piled on board. The big tech companies are salivating at purchasing the technology. Your friend has now offered you a million-dollar investment to support the startup. Let's call this first opportunity 'Hot Startup'.

The second opportunity is an easily rentable apartment in London's Mayfair, a desirable area with a combination of residential and business units. London's property prices are robust and were barely singed by the 2008 financial crisis and Brexit. This is because London remains the economic heart of Europe. Let's call this option 'London Apartment'.

Our third option is to buy $1 million worth of an index of the top 500 U.S. companies as decided and monitored by Standard & Poor's. We'll call this option 'S&P 500'.

For the sake of simplicity, let's assume you are buying each of these investments directly with no middlemen or brokers or pooling together with friends. It's just you who is making the decision. Now let's get check-listing using the Hot Startup, London Apartment and S&P 500 investment options as our guinea pigs.

Effort and monitoring

How much work will this investment take to complete? How much time per month will it take to monitor? How much might it cost to keep up? The first thing on the Superinvestar Checklist is the effort it will take to make and monitor the investment.

To get an investment over the finish line takes different levels of effort. In the case of the S&P 500, you'll probably have a brokerage app on your phone, or you can open one online in under ten minutes. Buying the S&P 500 is then a matter of a few clicks. Monitoring your index can be done constantly, although you probably shouldn't look at your phone that much. The S&P 500 is rebalanced by the researchers at Standard and Poor's quarterly, so if you're heavily invested, you could check what companies dropped out of the top 500 and what new ones were included to truly 'monitor' what you're invested in. But even if you don't monitor it, the 500 constituent companies will be beavering away, creating goods and services and hopefully expanding their market capitalization.

If you are looking to buy an apartment for rental income, it takes months to research and decide on a place to buy. Then you must reach a deal, prepare the accommodation, find a tenant and make sure they pay rent each month. The London Apartment option will need maintenance and upkeep, especially if the building is old. If the washing machine breaks, unless you have a good agent in place, it's going to be you who's running to fix things.

Now let's take the Hot Startup. In terms of effort, unless you know the space the company is starting up in, you might need to learn quite a lot about its technology. Investing will involve signing a few papers – not quite the touch of a button, but not too onerous. It could also be quite fun to get involved with other angel investors and advise the startup.

The monitoring part might get sticky, though. If you're a major investor, you may get a board seat. This would mean meetings and time blocked out of your diary. If you don't have a board seat, you will have to monitor how the company is doing. If the company struggles on any front, you will have the job of trying to get your friend as founder to change course. You will have to bring a lot to the table in terms of future investors, market knowledge and engagement with your friend. The Hot Startup would be high on monitoring.

Lockup and liquidity

How long will you be committing your money? What's the quickest length of time you can get it back? How easily can you get this money back if you need it? Lockup and liquidity are closely related, but different concepts. Both deal with how you're going to get your money back once you commit to an investment, but lockup is how long your money will be locked up for, which could be a practical measure in a contract or the reality of how a particular investment works, while liquidity is the time it will take to get your money back once you've pressed the 'sell' button.

In the case of the Hot Startup, the lockup will be a minimum of a few years. It's hard to ask for money back from a startup, and if you've given a friend $1 million for their startup, asking for it back will probably mean their business folding. You will essentially destroy your investment. A startup generally has terms to ensure it takes a long time to get your investment back. Your lockup time is high and your liquidity is low.

A London apartment bought today would take a minimum of three months to sell. You'd probably lose money from taxes and transaction fees, so if you're buying a property in London, you're making a three- to five-year commitment to break even. But it's nearly a sure bet you'll be able to sell it.

The S&P 500 can be bought and sold at will. You can buy in the morning and sell in the evening. There is a lockup of a few hours to overnight. Unless the market crashes badly, you will probably get your investment back for a few dollars in trading fees. Unless you're buying something super-exotic in the stock market, there's likely to be someone who will buy it off you.

It's worth looking at contractual clauses for every investment. P.E. funds might formally lock up your money for five to ten years, hedge funds for a year or more. The investment managers need the time to make their strategies work, so balance your need to access the money against the promised high returns. Investing is an art, not a science.

Diversification

Do you own a lot of the same type of investment already? Are you over-concentrated in any country, industry or asset type? This is probably the most important part of the Superinvestar Checklist.

I worked for Lehman Brothers from 2001–2002 and made and retained many friendships within the firm. I worked with normal people with families and mortgages and no source of wealth outside the monthly Lehman salary.

Lehman had an internal private wealth management team for elite investors. Employees could choose to have money managed by this part of the firm. Bonuses were generous, and if we took our bonuses in Lehman shares, we would get an even more generous uplift. Of course, many of the savvy employees took advantage of this and invested much of their wealth in company shares. It made sense for the employees to entrust their life savings to their employer. Well, at least it did until it didn't.

In August 2008, as the world watched Lehman Brothers' stock price collapse much of this wealth was either wiped out or tied up for a long, uncertain and horrendous period.

Think back to the year 2000. Google was two years old. Mark Zuckerberg was sixteen years old and still four years away from founding Facebook. The FT Global 500[15] is a list of the largest global companies put together by the Financial Times. Out of the top ten companies ranking in 2000 only one, Microsoft, has stayed on the top ten list as we approach the year 2020. In 2000 there were no Chinese companies, now there are two, Alibaba and Tencent. Intel, Pfizer and General Electric that dominated the top ten in 2000 are no longer market darlings. The market giveth and the market taketh away.

The lesson of diversification is to avoid scrambled eggs by not putting all your eggs in one basket. As usual with investing, nothing is straightforward, so we need to have several types of basket and many types of eggs.

Investment type

These would be the traditional asset allocation baskets: stocks and shares (equities), bonds (fixed income), real assets (houses, gold) and alternative investments such as venture capital and angel investing. The ice-cream

---

15   www.ft.com/ft500

sundae investing model in the previous chapter helps us picture this.

Industry

The next requirement is to diversify across industry sectors such as energy, automotive, technology, consumer goods, logistics... the list goes on. Global Industry Classification Standard (G.I.C.S.) is the standard investment-industry terminology for sectors.

Geography

Diversification also needs to span the world. You could invest in individual countries such as the United States, Canada and Mexico, or by world region – Asia, Europe, etc.

You generally have mature markets – North America and Europe. Emerging markets such as India and China are thought to be where the booming investors will drive growth in future decades. You also have frontier markets such as Morocco and Myanmar, where the economies are nascent in the stock-market sense, but could have huge payoffs for early investors.

Theme and style

The last way to diversify is by themes or styles of investing. Currently there is a lot of money chasing

A.I. and E.S.G. or sustainability investing. Styles that are popular are enhanced indexing, smart beta – where funds claim to be able to pick the better performing companies according to how their numbers are moving – and E.T.F.s that mimic a collection of companies.

Let's put our three guinea-pig investments to the test. The Hot Startup is heavy on technology, so the geographical location probably doesn't matter too much for this investment. There is a benefit for being in the Silicon Valley financing ecosystem, but the startup will pay higher salaries, rent, etc. But do you have any other angel investments? Are you going too heavy on the sprinkles? The technology focuses on A.I. for hospitals. Are you loading up too much on A.I., the success of which is yet to play out? Are you concentrating too much in the medical sector?

The London Apartment is a good investment if the London economy continues to boom, but if you live in London and are dependent on the U.K. economy for your business doing well, does it make sense to put more eggs in the same basket? Is your wealth already dependent on a lot of real estate? Do you hold a lot of rental real-estate assets that need looking after? Would you be better off diversifying into easier-to-manage virtual assets like shares in real-estate companies?

The S&P 500 only includes the 500 largest U.S. companies, so you miss out on those potential gems in

Europe or Asia. Industry-wise it is well diversified, but it does not benefit from any particular style or trend. The bet is on the long-term growth of the U.S. economy. Are you already heavily weighted towards the United States? The S&P 500 is a nice, solid basic index, but do you need to be a bit more exciting in looking for returns?

Expertise likes to build on expertise. It's the easiest thing in the world to make a second investment in an area you already know about. Silicon Valley entrepreneurs tend to sell their companies then put a lot of money into other startups. The oil industry is extremely complicated, so energy stock pickers will use their deep knowledge to pick multiple stocks in this sector. This is fine if you run an energy sector fund – that's what you're being paid for – but a choppy ride if you're doing it for your own wealth.

Even the cleverest and most concentrated of investors – the big multibillion-dollar funds that make *Wall Street Journal* front pages – tend to hold fifteen positions or more with only about 7% of their portfolio in their biggest and most optimistic bet. Professional value investors who spend their entire weeks (and weekends) poring over company reports advocate thirty to fifty holdings, so most of their bets are 2–3% of their portfolio. Mutual fund managers hold 100s of positions.

Go ahead and buy something you're confident will grow, but keep in mind how much of your net worth you're putting on one bet. Avoid scrambled eggs.

Floor

How much money can you lose? What's the worst-case scenario? How low can this investment go? The fourth item on the Superinvestar Checklist is the floor or worst-case scenario. How likely is it that you could lose all your money?

The Hot Startup could go big. It could be the next Amazon or Google. But most likely not. It might get acquired by a competitor or a larger company if it doesn't build the product and customers. That would involve a *real* risk that the value of your investment could go to zero.

The London Apartment is more robust. In the 2008 crisis, London housing took a battering, but soon recovered. Even after the announcement of Brexit, the prices held firm.

The S&P 500 is a bellwether of the economy. Even though it took its hits in 2008, the chance that the S&P will go to zero is small. If that did happen, we would have much more worrying things to think about, such as nuclear holocaust or a worldwide plague or zombie apocalypse.

Price

Price is what you pay; value is what you get.
— Warren Buffett

Are you paying too much for this? Are you paying a fair price or a low price? If the price is low, why is it low? How do you know what the 'right' price for this investment is?

The Hot Startup is the most difficult to value. Startups usually do not have revenues; the price you pay to buy a slice of them is purely speculative, based on what they might achieve as a valuation in the future. At each stage of the fund-raising process, the founders have a pre-money valuation, and after the funding round a post-money valuation. The valuation increase is dependent on how valuable the competing venture or angel investors perceive the startup to be.

A London Apartment option is a dream come true for many, but after years of booming prices, how much higher can they get? You want to buy at a fair valuation without assuming prices will forever keep going up. If you buy the apartment with a loan/mortgage, the rent you can charge has to exceed your monthly mortgage payment (and whatever other property expenses you have) for you to turn a profit. Real estate is deeply influenced by the gravitational economic force that is interest rates.

For the S&P 500 option, you want to buy low and sell high. The valuation of the largest companies shifts daily to emotions in the marketplace and the mood of the large asset managers. For example, the S&P 500 is revalued quarterly. If a company enters as the 500th company on the list, the funds and indexes that track the S&P 500 are immediately obligated to buy shares in the company to be compliant with the S&P 500 methodology and their agreements with investors. Nothing fundamental about the 500th company's revenues or customers has shifted, but its price has gone up due to increased demand.

What price are you paying for the large S&P 500 companies that everyone is paying attention to, such as Google or Amazon? Is their predicted tremendous growth already priced into the share price? When will you get out? Many of the largest companies will grow, but is it enough to justify the price you pay today?

Fees

How are the people selling you this investment incentivized? Are your interests aligned? What part of the returns will be eaten up by fees? Fees on fees on fees on fees. The financial industry runs on fees, and it makes sense to take a good look at where you will pay out over the years.

The F.C.A. – the U.K. financial watchdog – brought in strict rules to reduce the fees paid by ordinary investors and make them more transparent, but it still estimates that these investors pay 2.5–3%[16] of their portfolio in fees each year. Possibly more if they have sophisticated instruments they don't understand and bespoke financial advice. Nothing in investing is free, so check carefully. A lot of fees are hidden, and despite government efforts, they remain undisclosed and opaque. You have to trust your wealth manager to be working in your best interest. Sometimes by being the one client who asks questions about the fees, you will ensure that you get reasonable fee options.

The Hot Startup – if you are making a direct investment, there won't be fees. If you're investing in a venture fund, these usually charge a 2% management fee annually and a 20% performance fee on the increase in investment. The London Apartment will have transaction costs associated with it. The real estate agent will have to be paid a few percentage points in commission. The surveyors, lawyers and other checks will eat into your profit. The S&P 500 fees will all depend on how you're buying in. If it's through your online brokerage accounts such as TD Ameritrade or Hargreaves Lansdown, you'll pay a one-off fee for the transaction. Make sure this is a fixed fee rather than a percentage fee. It takes just as much effort and computing power to buy 100 shares as it does to buy 1,000 shares. If you're buying via your wealth manager, don't forget to factor in that they have

16   www.ft.com/content/56243606-6614-11e6-a08a-c7ac04ef00aa

already charged you to manage your assets and these fees will be an additional cost to you.

Why care about fees?

The U.S. government's watchdog, the S.E.C. Office of Investor Education and Advocacy, gives the example of a portfolio of $100,000 that earns 4% on average for twenty years. The portfolio will be worth $210,000 with annual fees of 0.25%, only $180,000 with a fee of 1.0%. That's a $30,000 difference on a relatively small amount.[17] As a consumer of investment services, you have a right to ask about fees so shop around for something that sits comfortably with you.

My clever friend T is a physician at a large hospital in California. He is married to another physician. The hospital introduced a pension scheme bringing in a well-known financial advisor. My friend asked me to look at their documents, saying he was happy because the only fees they charged were an overall management fee and he named a reasonable number just under the 1% mark.

The financial advisor hadn't mentioned that each of the funds my friend and his partner would be putting in to would charge their own fees too. On top of that, every time the funds bought or sold something

---

17   'How Fees and Expenses Affect Your Investment Portfolio', www.sec.gov/investor/alerts/ib_fees_expenses.pdf

within the fund, there would be transaction costs. Many banks make their money constantly buying and selling (churning) shares and bonds within funds they manage, the brokerage arms of the business taking the commissions for the trades.

Types of fees

One of the problems with fees is that many investors are unaware of the various types. They might be told about some, but not others. Look through this list and use it as an initial checklist (this is *not* an exhaustive list):

- Platform costs – costs to use any technological platform your investments might be based on.

- Foreign-exchange charges – if the fund you're invested in holds investments abroad, there will be foreign-exchange transfer charges.

- Transaction costs for underlying investments – the cost of buying the actual shares/bonds that make up individual funds.

- Expense ratio or internal fees – the cost of creating a fund.

- Investment advisory charges – the cost of an advisor telling you which fund to hold.

- Entry fees – costs when you initially buy an investment. Find out if these are billed to you or just taken out of your investment.

- Exit fees – costs associated with selling/leaving a fund, especially if you do so under a minimum period. Best to know about them before you invest.

- Annual custodian fee – annual charges to keep certain accounts open and in compliance with government rules.

- Commissions – fees paid to investment advisors and people giving financial advice to promote certain investments or brands. This is a sticky one to ask about, but you need to be satisfied with how the people advising you are being paid.

If you have other types of investments like hedge funds, P.E. or real estate, the scope of additional fees increases.

The main questions to ask about investment fees

Ask your financial advisor:

- Do you have a full schedule of fees you can share?

- Is everything listed? Refer to the list above.

- What fees are one-offs? Which fees are recurring annually?

- What fees are paid at the beginning of an investment?

- What fees are paid when you withdraw your money?

You can find a more detailed document:

- From the U.S. government: www.sec.gov/ investor/alerts/ib_fees_expenses.pdf
- From the U.K. government: www. moneyadviceservice.org.uk/en/articles/ guide-to-financial-adviser-fees

F.O.M.O.

Is there something about this investment that feels pressured? Are you trying to impress someone with it? Are you keeping up with what your friends are doing?

The Hot Startup is one where you have to watch out for F.O.M.O. You usually have a limited time to invest in a startup, sometimes just a few days. If friends you respect are going in, it's easy to follow them.

Startups are built on big ideas, and the fear of missing out on the next big moneymaker goes straight into the emotional brain. There is nothing that I can advocate for this, except using your gut check, a sense check. If you do angel investing, I would strongly advise you use a specialized checklist you've created for yourself.

The London Apartment can also see you succumbing to F.O.M.O. In normal market conditions when a piece of real estate comes on the market, it's usually only available for a few weeks. The person with the highest bid tends to win. Look at what price you're paying and make sure you consider how much F.O.M.O. is going on to help you stay realistic.

The S&P 500 has been around for decades, and some form of the stock market will be around long after any of us reading (or writing) this book is dead. People tend to have a feeling that they should have started investing and have missed out on returns by not going in earlier. It's worth minding that you don't try to 'catch up' by going into riskier investments.

Taxes

If you're starting with the end in mind, taxes are a good problem to have. They mean you have grown your money and are in the position of owing the government for the increase in your capital. Worrying about taxes is also a good sign that you live in a stable political environment where the government is effective enough to collect taxes.

The tax tail wagging the investment dog

When I'm working with my investment coaching clients, I'll often ask them why they went into a certain investment. The answer tends to be that they were told it was a tax-efficient vehicle. This is the tax tail wagging the investment dog. It's fine to minimize paying taxes, but...

At the end of the day, tax vehicles and ownership structures are expensive to set up and will require annual updates and filings. Over the decades, is it going to be worth all the accountants' and legal fees, not to mention the hassle? If a wealth manager or private bank is setting up the structures for you, are you ever going to be able to move your money out of their control without replicating a costly structure?

The Hot Startup shares could sell for an enormous amount someday, in which case you'll owe taxes. The U.K. government has encouraged angel investing since 2012 by giving generous tax breaks[18] on startup investments, so if you live in the U.K., it's always worth exploring these options.

The London Apartment might attract taxes you aren't aware of. Recently the government made changes to discourage buy-to-let landlords, which caught many investors off guard. In the United States, there are different tax consequences. Certain real estate classes in inner cities or for the public good can have added tax benefits.

---

18 www.gov.uk/topic/business-tax/investment-schemes

The S&P 500, if it goes up, will attract taxes on any gains. Make sure your investment manager knows you want a tax-efficient or tax-harvesting structure. These vary widely from asset manager to asset manager. You cannot control the market, but you can choose to retain as much of your gains as you can. Individual funds can also differ in how they are taxed, so *please* ask about the tax implications of any investment you make. In the United States, if you hold shares for over a year, your tax liability goes down. It's always worth checking with a sensible accountant you're paying to advise you directly independently of your wealth manager.

Always ask the question about tax liabilities in case you do win big with an investment. Remember to have the investment dog wagging the tax tail, not the other way around.

Long-term return

The last item on the essential Superinvestar Checklist is the return on investment (R.O.I.). I purposely placed it last since it's what most investors ask me about first.

The Hot Startup has the potential to generate the biggest returns. The next Google could see your investment multiply thousands of times over. Even a startup with a decent exit, such as being bought by Google, could net you your money many times over.

The London Apartment could provide you with both a rental income and an appreciation. The London market has been sound for the last few decades, but if you're buying elsewhere, you might want to check that you will always be able to rent the property out, and that prices are fair and going up. Real estate won't give you the returns a startup could, but at the end of the day, you will own something that can be rented out for income or lived in.

The S&P 500 over the long term will give you returns. The largest 500 American companies are going to do well, and buying an index ensures you're always up to date with them. But there will be blips and crashes, so this is only something to think about for the long term.

An overview

Let's go back now and summarize the three investments. Remember, there is no perfect investment. Using a simple checklist gets us away from gut feel while making sure we don't get caught up in analysis paralysis and complicated models that are best left to the professional math nerds.

These are my thoughts on the three different investments.

Superinvestar Checklist	Hot Startup	London Apartment	S&P 500
Effort and monitoring	High	High	Low
Lockup and liquidity	Low	Medium	High
Diversification	Medium	Medium	Medium
Floor	Poor	Great	Good
Price	Good	High	High
Fees	Good	Too high	Great
F.O.M.O.	Oops	Oops	Oops
Taxes	Great	Good	Poor
Long-term return	Very high/ zero	Decent	Decent but choppy

As you can see, there is no correct answer that this model spits out with an easy yes or no. Hopefully, you can use it to think through the next opportunity that is put in front of you. I welcome you to customize, experiment and own your investing checklists.

Further steps

- Do the investment managers you engage with have checklists? Are they willing to share them?

- If the investment managers you use don't use checklists, how do they manage their decision process? Do they score investments or use another technique?

- Diversification – is there an area you are overconcentrated in? Does this make you uncomfortable or is it a tactical decision?

- F.O.M.O. – the fear of missing out. Is there an investment decision you've made because your friends and colleagues were all getting into it?

- Read the book *The Checklist Manifesto* by Atul Gawande.

9
Conclusion

I am not God. In the Church of Investing, I wouldn't even make it to minor sainthood. I am a devout worshipper, though, and I love investing. I enjoy watching my clients have a series of lightbulb moments, and I hope you have found this book useful.

By now, I'm sure it's clear to you that the Superinvestar Framework is just a friendly tweaking of what every major asset manager must think about. Control is about how you divvy up your time and who the decision makers are. Confidence is about finding high-quality investment opportunities from good sources. Calm is the behavioral finance bit, keeping decision-making within the logical brain. Clarity is about asset allocation, and checklists are risk management. Those terms would be recognizable to the investment managers of Mayfair, the heart of London's hedge-fund district where I work.

Mayfair on weekdays is the home of a thousand and one investment managers and related businesses. We are not a colorful or attention-grabbing bunch, but for a week every September, we become the epicenter of the London Fashion Week. The mood changes with taxis ferrying models and designers doused in perfume, feathers and silks (the high heels mean they can't walk).

My favorite Fashion Week memory is from a few years ago. As I rounded a corner on Berkeley Square, I found myself staring down the lenses of what seemed like a hundred paparazzi cameras, all pointing at me. But their attention only lasted about half a second. They realized I was a nobody and the cameras promptly went down. I'm still wondering what gave it away. The flat shoes? The never-was-in-fashion handbag? The full-fat hot chocolate in my hand?

As out of synch as the investing world and the fashion world seem outwardly, we have a fundamental principle in common: to sell our products, we bring out a new collection every season. Fashion designers change colors, take hems up and down and tweak handbag shapes. Investment firms create products based on the latest hot technologies and societal trends, and there will be great pressure to pick and present the most fashionable. It's a juggling act for those of us on the decision-making side of where to allocate capital.

Back in the early 2000s, when there was money to be made in banking, it was acceptable for twenty-something hotshot investment types to take a few months off to pursue kitesurfing or world traveling, and then come back for their next gig. Jobs in finance were easy to get. The trick was to be 'let go', not fired for incompetence. That way you would be paid a parting bonus, usually three to six months' salary, twelve months if you were lucky. Financial institutions regularly culled the bottom 5–10% of their performers, so managers were always looking for additional people to fire.

If you were a young fund manager who wanted to underperform your way to a beach in Barbados, there were two main ways of achieving this:

- Show up inconsistently, miss meetings, be great at keeping on top of things one month and not so good the next.

- Not execute on your project plan. Push things forward incrementally, but not with any boldness.

Hmmm. Now ask yourself these two questions about your own investments:

- Do you show up consistently to manage your investments?

- Do you have a solid and active plan for where you want to be financially that you push forward consistently?

If the answer to either of those questions is no, then maybe it's time to rethink your role as your fund manager. You have two options – you could either fire yourself, i.e. outsource the role, or like any good employer, you could give yourself a second chance. Often it seems like cloning yourself is the only way to get the investing to-do list done.

We began this book looking at the three Hindu Gods of Creation, Preservation and Destruction. Now let's turn to my favorite Hindu God, Nataraja. He is the Lord of the Dance; the master of the cosmic balancing act with his many arms keeping the world stable. Perhaps he is a good symbol for how each of us must weigh up our decisions and keep our investments stable.

Ten timeless investing principles

1. **Investor or trader.** Decide if you are an investor or trader. Investors invest for the long term. Traders speculate for the short term. It's alright to pick either strategy, just not for the same investment.

2. **Low hanging fruit.** Increase your investment returns by striving to minimize fees and other costs. Technology is constantly creating innovative investment products with lower fees.

3. **Avoid scrambled eggs.** Don't put all your investment eggs in one basket. Diversify across geographies, industries and investing themes. Practice sensible asset allocation across stocks, bonds and 'real' assets.

4. **Prepare for panic.** Mr. Market swings from euphoria to depression and back again. Nobody, including the most elite investors, can predict the future accurately. Avoid trying to time the market. Have a plan for a downturn.

5. **Define risk for yourself.** Is risk the up and down gyrations of the market, or is it the permanent loss of capital? Look at both the quality of the investment and the price. Buy the best possible quality at the lowest price. Try to buy with a margin of safety.

6. **Tame your brain.** Investing decisions are ideally made in the logical part of our brain, but many of us are caught out by reacting impulsively. Educate yourself, learn consistently and resist acting from F.O.M.O.

7. **Liquidity and lockup.** Consider how quickly you can get your money back. How easily can you sell the investment (liquidity)? How long is your money tied up in the investment (lockup)?

8. **Enjoy the process.** Investing is deeply pleasurable to its best practitioners. Cultivate an abundance mindset – we enjoy luxuries today that royalty couldn't access 100 years ago. Billions of people will see their quality of life improve in the next decade. Invest accordingly.

9. **Automation.** Harness technology to automate every investment process you can. Save automatically. Rebalance automatically. Use technology to find the best investments for you automatically.

10. **Imitation.** The best investors write books and blogs and give interviews. You can follow their teachings for almost no cost. Develop your circle of investing competence and outsource the rest.

Further Reading

Beyer, Charlotte (2017) *Wealth Management Unwrapped, Revised and Expanded: Unwrap What You Need to Know and Enjoy the Present.* John Wiley & Sons.

Bhansali, Rupal (2019) *Non-Consensus Investing: Being Right When Everyone Else Is Wrong.* Columbia Business School Publishing.

Bogle, John C. (2012) *The Clash of the Cultures: Investment vs. Speculation.* John Wiley & Sons.

Bogle, John C. (2017) *The Little Book of Common Sense Investing: The Only Way to Guarantee Your Fair Share of Stock Market Returns.* John Wiley & Sons.

Chan, Ronald (2012) *The Value Investors: Lessons from the World's Top Fund Managers.* John Wiley & Sons.

Cunningham, Lawrence A. (2013) *The Essays of Warren Buffett: Lessons for Investors and Managers.* John Wiley & Sons.

Dalio, Ray (2018) *Principles for Navigating Big Debt Crises: The Archetypal Big Debt Cycle / Detailed Case Studies / Compendium of 48 Cases.* Bridgewater.

Dorsey, Pat (2008) *The Little Book That Builds Wealth: The Knockout Formula for Finding Great Investments.* John Wiley & Sons.

Faber, Mebane T. and Eric Richardson (2011) *The Ivy Portfolio: How to Invest Like the Top Endowments and Avoid Bear Markets.* John Wiley & Sons.

Fisher, Philip A. (1996) *Common Stocks and Uncommon Profits and Other Writings.* Wiley.

García Paramés, Francisco (2018) *Investing for the Long Term.* John Wiley & Sons.

Gawande, Atul (2011) *The Checklist Manifesto: How to Get Things Right.* Profile.

Greenblatt, Joel (2010) *The Little Book That Still Beats the Market.* John Wiley & Sons.

Greenblatt, Joel (1999) *You Can be a Stock Market Genius: Uncover the Secret Hiding Places of Stock Market Profits*. Fireside.

Hagstrom, Robert G. (2013) *Investing: The Last Liberal Art*. Columbia University Press.

Hsu, Chiente (2013) *Rule Based Investing: Designing Effective Quantitative Strategies for Foreign Exchange, Interest Rates, Emerging Markets, Equity Indices and Volatility*. Financial Times/ Prentice Hall.

Ilmanen, Antti (2012) *Expected Returns on Major Asset Classes*. CFA Institute.

Kahneman, Daniel (2012) *Thinking, Fast and Slow*. Penguin.

Klarman, Seth (1991) *Margin of Safety: Risk-Averse Value Investing Strategies for the Thoughtful Investor*. Harper Business.

Kroijer, Lars (2014) *Investing Demystified: How to Invest Without Speculation and Sleepless Nights*. FT Press.

Lo, Andrew W. (2017) *Adaptive Markets: Financial Evolution at the Speed of Thought*. Princeton University Press.

Lynch, Peter (2000) *One Up on Wall Street: How to Use What You Already Know to Make Money in The Market.* Simon & Schuster.

Marks, Howard (2018) *Mastering the Market Cycle: Getting the odds on your side.* Nicholas Brealey Publishing.

Marks, Howard (2011) *The Most Important Thing: Uncommon Sense for the Thoughtful Investor.* Columbia University Press.

Mihaljevic, John (2013) *The Manual of Ideas: The Proven Framework for Finding the Best Value Investments.* John Wiley & Sons.

Montier, James (2010) *The Little Book of Behavioral Investing: How Not to be Your Own Worst Enemy.* John Wiley & Sons.

Oldfield, Richard (2007) *Simple But Not Easy: An Autobiographical and Biased Book About Investing.* Doddington Publishing.

Pabrai, Mohnish (2007) *The Dhandho Investor: The Low-Risk Value Method to High Returns.* John Wiley & Sons.

Phelps, Thomas William (2015) *100 to 1 in the Stock Market: A Distinguished Security Analyst Tells How to Make More of Your Investment Opportunities.* Echo Point Books & Media.

Risso-Gill, Christopher (2011) *There's Always Something to Do: The Peter Cundill Investment Approach.* McGill-Queen's University Press.

Robbins, Tony (2014) *Money: Master the Game, 7 Simple Steps to Financial Freedom.* Simon & Schuster.

Schroeder, Alice (2008) *The Snowball: Warren Buffett and the Business of Life.* Bloomsbury Publishing.

Shearn, Michael (2011) *The Investment Checklist: The Art of In-Depth Research.* John Wiley & Sons.

Spier, Guy ((2014) *The Education of a Value Investor: My Transformative Quest for Wealth, Wisdom, and Enlightenment.* St. Martin's Press.

Swensen, David F. (2005) *Unconventional Success: A Fundamental Approach to Personal Investment.* Free Press.

Thomas, Guy (2011) *Free Capital: How 12 private investors made millions in the stock market.* Harriman House.

Thorndike William N. (2012) *Outsiders: Eight Unconventional C.E.O.s and Their Radically Rational Blueprint for Success.* Harvard Business Review Press.

Tyson, Eric (2014) *Investing for Dummies.* For Dummies.

Acknowledgments

I would like to offer my thanks to:

- Professor Thomas Kailath and Anu Maitra

- Anu Choraria and Sanjeev Choraria for housing my venture

- Sanjay Chandiram – an entrepreneurial inspiration

- Su Robotti and Bob Robotti for their support

- Dominic Fisher of Thistledown Investment Management

- Dhiraj Mukherjee and Rachel Mukherjee

- Akshata Murty for her support

- Professor Narayan Naik of London Business School for the opportunities to speak to his students

- Professor John Hennessey and Narayana Murty – leaders by example

- Norman Rentrop for inviting me to speak in Omaha

- Dan DiBartimoleo for so generously sharing his inimitable knowledge of the markets

- Chandini Munjal Arora

- Dr. John Walker and Guilda Navidi-Walker

- John Mihaljevic of M.O.I. Global

- Daniel Priestley of Dent Global

- Paul Varotsis and Agnes Varotsis

- Susan Spiller and Dr Linda Hickman for countless words of wisdom

- Arne Lim – Math opens doors

- Samuel Samson for his accounting expertise

- Danilo Santiago of Rational Investment Methodology

- Whitney Tilson, Ciccio Azzollini and Valeria Paloscia for including me in VIS Trani

- Shai Dardashti of the Casulo Group

- Monika Strum and Karin Bayer

- Christian Freischütz of Value School

- Robert Leitz of Iolite Partners

- Ashith Kampani

- Rupert Von Eisenhardt Goodwin of the London Quant Group

- Robert Macrae at the L.S.E. Systemic Risk Centre

- Ed Fishwick at Blackrock

- Antonia Lim

- Dr. Rajeev Krishnamoorthy

- Dr. Jeannie Kahwajy

- Lorna Wade for invaluable research pointers

- Baldwin Berges

- Liz Boyle

- Tom Sebastian

- Dave Nile

- Sigrun Gudjonsdottir

- Jill Lyons

- Jon Boylan

- Karin Wiberg for professionalizing my text

- The Stanford Community in London: Mark Dominik, Dr. Cyrus Hirjibehedin, Eric Jonsson, Gretchen Welch, Lisa Cirenza, Alison Kemmis-Price, Diane Stewart, Ed Tran

- Most of my thanks for the day-to-day invaluable friendship and support for which I am most grateful goes to: **Malavika Solanki, Meghna Abraham, Archana Roy, Pauline Chung, Brian Preston** and, last but definitely not least, **Elena Terzieva** for chimp wrangling

The Author

Mallika serves as an investment coach for individuals and families. Her own painful past in learning to manage investments led her to create a long-term focused, value-oriented education platform.

Born in India, Mallika moved to Silicon Valley as a child. Graduating from Palo Alto High School and attending Stanford University in the 1990s, she then worked for several startups and had a ring-side seat of the rise and fall of the nineties' tech bubble.

Quantitatively trained, she began her career as a programmer in Silicon Valley and has worked at Lehman Brothers, Trucost (now S&P), M.S.C.I. Barra and several funds in Wall Street and London's The City.

She is past president and a board member of the Stanford Club of Great Britain, a member of the Stanford Angels Network U.K., and served a two-year term as a board member on the London School of Economics Alumni Committee. For ten years, she worked in sustainability investing, including renewable energy and governance issues. She has also worked for a premier index investing provider and risk manager and has a good handle on how indexes are created and implemented.

Throughout her career, elite investors have sought her out as a clear and sensible sounding board. Mallika educates her clients through clear and practical measures based on timeless principles and long-term investing. She has been a guest speaker at London Business School on value investing and Stanford University on sustainable investing.

Mallika has a B.A. from Stanford University, an M.Sc. from the London School of Economics and has completed the Investment Management Programme at London Business School. She was awarded the Women's Club of Palo Alto scholarship for one graduating senior and the Stanford Alumni Association's Award of Merit in 2013.

You can email her at
me@mallika-invests.com

You can follow her investing notes at
mallika-invests.com

Printed in Great Britain
by Amazon

33097522R00115